Dealing With

Doubts in Islam

For Those That Want to Clear Their Doubts Before
Converting to Islam or Suffering From Whispers of Satan

From The Sincere Seeker Collection

All praise & gratitude is for God, the worthy One;
to Whom belongs whatever is in the Heavens & Earth.

In the name of Allah, the Most Compassionate, Most Merciful. All praises are due to Allah; we praise Him; we seek His Help; we seek His Forgiveness and seek His Guidance. We seek refuge in Allah from the evil in our souls and the wickedness of our deeds. For whomever Allah Guides, there is none to lead him astray. And for whomever He allows going astray, there is none to guide him. I bear witness that there is none worthy of worship except Allah, for whom there is no partner. And I bear witness that Muhammad is His servant and last and final Messenger.

Table of Contents

About Me

It is imperative to note that I am not a scholar of the religion of Islam with any official diplomas in religious studies. I developed The Sincere Seeker platform and wrote this book along with others in my spare time after graduating with a secular degree in the United States. My work is not comparable to Islam's more learned and knowledgeable scholars. My intention in creating The Sincere Seeker platform and writing this book is to use what God has gifted me to contribute to society and teach others about God the Glorious, the Holy Quran, the way of Islam, and the Prophet Muhammad PBUH.

The Young Age of Aisha
When She Married Prophet Muhammad PBUH

A common accusation and attempt to defame the beautiful character of Prophet Muhammad PBUH comes in contemplation of his judgment and ethics in marrying his wife, Aisha R.A, given that she was of a young age. Authentic narrations of Aisha R.A. state that she was six years old when the marriage took place in Mecca and nine years old when she moved into the house of Prophet Muhammad PBUH in Medina and consummated her marriage.

Aisha was the daughter of Prophet Muhammad PBUH's best friend, Abu Bakr R.A, who stood by Prophet Muhammad PBUH when others did not. Abu Bakr R.A. was the first man to accept the message of Islam and stood as a source of continuous support for Prophet Muhmmad PBUH throughout his journey of spreading the message of God to the people.

The attempt to defame the character of Prophet Muhammad PBUH for his marriage of Aisha R.A at a young age fell flat, like other attempts to attack his character. The controversy regarding the age of Aisha is a recent phenomenon—one that people had never had an issue with in the past, and for a good reason. During the lifetime of Prophet Muhammad

PBUH, his enemies would attack his character by calling him a sorcerer, a madman, a magician, a soothsayer, and much more, but they never mentioned the fact that he married someone of a young age.

Why didn't his enemies lodge a fact that would assist them in defaming and attacking the character of Prophet Muhammad PBUH, you ask? Because the age of Aisha R.A. at that time and place was deemed acceptable and the norm for marriageable women. Muslim historians who reported the story of Prophet Muhammad PBUH's marriage to Aisha R.A. never felt the need to justify her age because, at that time, some young ladies did marry. Aisha R.A. had been engaged to someone else before Prophet Muhammad PBUH, which tells us that she was old enough for marriage at that time and place.

Taking our current-day 21st-century cultural norms and projecting them onto the auspices of 7th-century Arabian society is not fair nor logical; in fact, it is considered a fallacy of presentism. One should not judge a person who lived more than 1400 years ago by today's standards, especially when doing something acceptable and normal at their time. Note each society has its own set of norms.

Throughout history, different cultures and ethnicities set different ages considered appropriate for marriage. The people in Arabia in the 7th century were married off early because, in the hot climate of the Arabia desert, young boys and girls matured at an early age, given that they had to assume family responsibilities. The typical age of marriage today in some countries is 13-15. In 12th-century Europe, some young girls would marry at the age of nine or ten. We shouldn't judge people of the past for marrying spouses of a young age, just like we wouldn't judge famous figures of history for owning slaves because it was accepted at that time as the norm.

Islam does not specify a minimum age for marriage. The requirement to marry someone is that they must be mentally and physically ready for the union. The phrase "mentally ready" means they are prepared to

3

shoulder the responsibility of motherhood and fulfill the duties of raising a family. Being physically prepared implies that one has reached the state of puberty. Islam looks at the local customs and traditions of the land at that time and place. The age of consent for marriage will vary depending on time, place, culture, and society. A particular 12-year-old may be ready for marriage, whereas a person of 24 years may not. Some lifespans ran only 30 to 40 years, so they would marry early to accommodate an abbreviated lifetime. One can argue that the 16-year-old of today is mentally equivalent to the 10-year-old of the past. The age of marriage in many Islamic countries today is 18.

It's imperative to note that because Prophet Muhmmad PBUH married Aisha R.A. at a young age, she lived many years after the death of her husband and dedicated her life to teaching others about the religion of Islam and Prophet Muhammad PBUH. Many of the companions of the Prophet PBUH came to her to gain a better understanding and clarity of Islamic rulings. She stands among the greatest scholars of Islam, who narrated more than two thousand Hadiths (saying of the Prophet PBUH), providing us with insights into Prophet Muhammad PBUH's behavior inside the home and how he dealt with his wives, how he slept, and his other actions inside the house.

Aisha R.A. was very fortunate to marry the best person who ever lived. She was pleased with her life, loved her husband, and never complained. Their marriage was based on love, compassion, and mercy. Aisha R.A. narrated many tender details regarding their romance. Among the many beautiful narrations, Aisha R.A shared was the love and tenderness Prophet Muhammad PBUH would display to her. She told how he would insist that she drink from a cup first, then drink from the same spot where Aisha R.A would place her lips.

Their marriage was based on God's command. Aisha R.A narrated that the Angel Gabriel came to Prophet Muhammad PBUH with the image of her on a piece of green silk cloth and said, *"This is your wife in this world and next."* (At-Tirmidhi). It's only logical to accept that God made the right decision, as He is All-Wise. It's also important to note that many of the women Prophet Muhammad PBUH married were older divorcees; indeed, Aisha was the only virgin.

From a biblical perspective, Mary was twelve when she married Joseph, who was ninety years old. But this is a Christian viewpoint that Muslims do not believe. According to Church fathers, Rebekah was three years old when she married Isaac. A second early source states her age as ten.

Islamic scholars do not believe we should replicate the standard age of marriage of the past in today's world. Muslim scholars state that a minimum age of consent could be imposed in modern times and places.

If God Exists, Why Does He Allow Evil, Pain, Suffering, and Sickness?

Throughout history, a single question has plagued humanity; a question often asked about an issue that all Abrahamic religions face. If an All-Powerful God, who is All-Knowing, All-Seeing, All-Hearing, Loving, Most-Merciful, and All-Just in control of All things and matters, exists, then why do people experience evil, pain, and suffering in this world? Why must we contend with sickness, natural disasters, starvation, war, calamities, corruption, and killings? If God is Most-Merciful, All-Loving, All-Good, and All-Just, why does He allow such atrocities to happen?

The existence of evil ranks among the top reasons people reject the concept of religion or the belief in a Higher Power. This concept is known as the "problem of evil." Many have concluded that God could not exist because of the presence of evil; if He does exist, He is a cruel, unjust God who enjoys seeing people suffer and in pain. They summarize that such a God is not worth worshipping if He is unaware, uncaring, and incapable of removing and controlling evil elements.

People who reject God because they cannot grapple with the problem of evil do not adequately understand the conditions of darkness and pain. They reject God because of their lack of understanding. The decision to disbelieve the existence of God only adds more confusion, leading to the emergence of questions as to why we were created, where we are destined to go, etc.

An atheist that rejects God removes God from the equation, but suffering still exists. Disbelieving only eliminates the quality and significance of the suffering and no longer gives it purpose or meaning. One could have suffered their whole life, only to end up in their grave eternally with no justice or recompense for what they had endured, and those who committed evil can get away with their misdeeds. However, with God in the equation, suffering has meaning, and the victims and the oppressed eventually receive justice in this world or the next. Without God in the picture, they may not. The fact that evil exists does not negate the existence of God.

The Angels first asked the question of evil upon God, the Almighty's announcement that He was creating a new form of beings called humans.

"And [mention, O Muhammad], when your Lord said to the angels, Indeed, I will make upon the Earth a successive authority" (Quran 2:30)

The Angels responded with a question:

"...They said, 'Will You place upon it one who causes corruption therein and sheds blood, while we declare Your praise and You?" (Quran 2:30)

God answered:

"...Indeed, I know that which you do not know" (Quran 2:20)

Although God did not explain nor rationalize the answer to their question, the Angels were satisfied with this response; this is owing to their complete humility before, trust in, and faith in God's Wisdom and Knowledge while recognizing His Wisdom as Perfect and without flaws.

7

The Angels did not assume God's Wisdom was incorrect simply because they could not understand nor comprehend that Wisdom. Humans never will understand the reason behind the world's pain and suffering, as our limited, finite minds cannot comprehend God's logic. However, the fact that our intellectual capacity cannot understand and evaluate the Wisdom behind pain and suffering does not nullify that Wisdom. How can we judge the situation or God without attaining the necessary information to do so? God states in the Quran:

"...And mankind has not been given of knowledge except a little" (Quran 17:85)

As humans, we can understand the Wisdom behind pain and suffering only on a general level. We have no right to question our Creator, as everything belongs to Allah, the Glorious, including us, and to Him, we will return. Whereas hardship, pain, and suffering exist in this world, their occurrence is the exception, not the rule. For example, generally, many people spend most of their lives enjoying health and only feel sick occasionally. And overall, Muslims disbelieve the concept of pure evil. Most things God has created are purely good in essence or possess a balance of good and evil. Nothing is purely evil, with no inherent goodness. Whereas evil can dominate more than good sometimes in everyday life, everything holds some element of good.

Every evil is good in some aspects; for instance, while sickness may harm the body temporally from one angle, illness also strengthens the immune system and teaches one patience with the healing process. Similarly, whereas volcanos can cause grave harm, they rejuvenate the ecosystem that facilitates life. Without volcanos, we could not grow food—as this natural phenomenon spews out minerals, resulting in rich fertile soil. One person's calamity can be another person's blessing; for instance, when one person loses a job, another person finds a new occupation.

A balance of good and evil is needed for both to exist. Poor and hungry people need to exist for charity and generosity to balance and benefit them. How can a person be generous if no charitable beneficiaries are available to assist? How can forgiveness occur when there is no offense to forgive? How can one learn patience without the perception of evil and calamities that test one's patience?

Similarly, following natural disasters, humanity shows generosity and support by sending medical assistance, food, cash donations, etc., to those affected. A negative occurrence can be followed by positive results to be manifested. Pain and suffering are blessings in disguise. God loves the good generated from the perception of evil.

Also, we need the existence of evil to recognize and appreciate good. When deprived of something valuable, we feel and appreciate all the more God's appreciation and blessings. One needs to experience hardship to value better times. Sometimes, one must fall ill to appreciate good health or suffer poverty to appreciate substance. Sometimes it's only in the darkness that one recognizes and appreciates the light. Hardship also helps us realize and ponder God's attributes, such as *The Healer* when we are sick or *The Protector* when we are in danger.

God does not love evil. Among the many pearls of Wisdom regarding pain and suffering, and probably the most important, is that trial and tribulation lead people back to God. Sometimes through tough times, people return and reconnect to their Lord in a show of desperation and with the utmost sincere prayers and supplications. Any calamity that brings one back to their Lord is not a true disaster; instead, it is a blessing in disguise. In times of tragedy, one increases his expressions of repentance, humility, and supplication, recognizing that he needs the Almighty.

"And when affliction touches man, he calls upon Us, whether lying on his side or sitting or standing; but when We remove from him his affliction, he continues in disobedience as if he had never called upon Us to remove an affliction that touched him. Thus, is made pleasing to the transgressors that which they have been doing" (Quran 10:12)

God can create any World He desires, including a World with no evil and suffering, and that place called Paradise exists. However, God, the Glorious, gave humanity the freedom of choice and free will. If He did not allow harm to occur, He would deprive society of free will. Since life is a test, this test would be meaningless without the free will given to humanity to take it. Sometimes, people in society act in evil ways as a consequence of free will. A creation of God that doesn't commit sin and evil exists called the Angel. God is not the direct cause of these acts of evil. Instead, He is the One who allows and wills it to happen for the greater good and for reasons we may or may not understand. God has provided us with free will to test us.

Among the essential justifications behind perceived evil is that life is a test for humanity, filled with many trials and tribulations.

"He who created death and life to test you as to which of you is best in deed — and He is the Exalted in Might, the Forgiving" (Quran 67:2)

These tests reveal a person's faith in and loyalty to God. God states:

"Do the people think that they will be left to say, 'We believe' and they will not be tried? But We have certainly tried those before them, and Allah will surely make evident those who are truthful, and He will surely make evident the liars" (Quran 29:2–3)

In another verse, God states:

"Or do you think that you will enter Paradise while such trial has not yet come to you as came to those who passed on before you? They were touched by poverty and hardship and were shaken until even their messenger, and those who believed with him said, 'When is the help of Allah?' Unquestionably, the help of Allah is near" (Quran 2:214)

In another Verse, God states:

"And We will surely test you with something of fear and hunger and a loss of wealth and lives and fruits, but give good tidings to the patient" (Quran 2:155)

According to the Holy Quran, evil deeds performed by humanity result in punishments here on Earth. Every act of suffering in this world is a fraction of what society has afflicted upon the Earth.

"Corruption has appeared throughout the land and sea by reason of what the hands of people have earned so He may let them taste part of the consequence of what they have done that perhaps they will return to righteousness" (Quran 30:41)

God references the fact that many past nations have been destroyed due to their evil actions and acts of disobedience.

"So, We took retribution from them, and We drowned them in the sea because they denied Our signs and were heedless of them" (Quran 7:136)

Among the many pearls of wisdom inherent in the perception of evil is the fact that God loves to forgive, as He is the Most-Merciful, the All-Forgiving. But for forgiveness to occur, there must be sins and sinners to forgive.

The protestation of human pain, suffering, misfortune, and hardship faced by innocent people and the claim that "life is unfair" are legitimate complaints, but only if belief in the Hereafter is denied and neglected. For any injustice in this world ever committed, justice will be served in the Hereafter. We will all face an afterlife, a Judgment Day, upon which justice will be served, and everyone will be compensated for their lifetime worth of actions. The evildoers will be punished for their sins, and the oppressed will be compensated and rewarded for their patience.

"And never think that Allah is unaware of what the wrongdoers do. He only delays them for a Day when eyes will stare in horror" (Quran 14:42)

This world never was intended to be a perfect place devoid of hardship. Some innocent babies die in infancy, but remember that life is given to us as a gift we did not deserve to receive. If a baby dies at an early age, it was the intention of God to will that baby to move on to the next life. We all come complete with an expiration date in this world, and we will live eternally in the next life. The fact that a baby died early does not negate the existence of a higher power that created the baby.

With great trials and patience come great rewards. If one were to measure the suffering of this world against the blessings of the Hereafter, what does 20, 40, 60, 80, or 100 years of suffering hold against an eternity of bliss?

We learn from a Hadith of the Prophet PBUH that on the day of judgment, a believer that lived a life of pain and suffering in this world will be dipped into a paradise for only a moment and asked, O, son of Adam, did you ever suffer any hardships or distress in your life? And they would respond, No, by God, I did not once see any hardship or distress. After entering Paradise for a moment, it would cause the person who had lived a life of pain and suffering to forget all their torment and travails. Those who did not believe in God and lived a life of pleasure in this world will soon forget all the joy and happiness they experienced the moment they are dipped into hellfire.

Muslims believe an ideal life without pain and suffering awaits them in the next world, not this one. This world is a stepping stone to the afterlife, leading you to Paradise or Hellfire.

Through the successful passing of tests, trials, and tribulations, God raises one's rankings. It is for this reason that God tests those He Loves. When calamity befalls a Muslim, God expiates a percentage of their sins. When a person who was patient in life sees their misfortunes on the Day of Judgment and receives the reward derived from this patience, they would wish that a more major calamity had struck them.

The Holy Quran offers different remedies for coping with hardship, such as faith, prayer, patience, trust, and reliance on God. Those who submit to Allah and utilize these remedies will find contentment and surety as they face their trials and tribulations. One must recognize that God will not place them in a situation they cannot manage.

"Allah does not burden a soul except with that within its capacity..." (Quran 2:286)

Realize that in the face of every hardship one faces, God has given the requirements to handle the situation and pass the test associated with it, or else He would not have placed that person in that difficulty. And realize that no harm can befall anyone except by the permission and Will of the Almighty. God states:

"Say, 'Never will we be struck except by what Allah has decreed for us; He is our protector' And upon Allah let the believers rely upon" (Quran 9:51)

A person of faith has a different attitude than those without faith regarding calamities. One with faith in God has surety and contentment in their heart, knowing that life is full of tests and trials, and with time and patience, matters will improve, and they will be rewarded. And remember, my dear brother or sister, what your Lord has promised:

"For indeed, with hardship will be ease. Indeed, with hardship will be ease" (Quran 94:5–6)

If God Preordained Everything,
Why Should I be held Accountable?

The last pillar of the Islamic faith, one that every Muslim believes, is the concept of Al-Qadr, which closely translates to predestination or pre-ordainment (sometimes translated as predestination/Divine Decree, destiny, or fate). When one believes in the tenet of Al-Qadr, translated as "Divine Decree," they affirm that everything--good or bad--that happens in their life emanates from God the Almighty and is something He willed to happen. Al-Qadr, in Arabic, translates to mean to measure, to determine, to assess, to decide, to judge. In the context of religion, the term means "Divine determined measurements and sustenance for everyone and everything, in accordance with His Wisdom and Power." God states in his Book:

Indeed, all things We created with predestination (Quran 54:49)

God the Almighty, being All-Knowing and All-Wise, knows what we have done in the past, what we are doing now, and what we will do in the future— even before our birth. After all, can God be God if He doesn't know everything, including the future? Whereas humanity has the free will to make their own choices, everything happens only and directly through God's Will and Power.

Before discussing the idea that if God preordained everything, why should we be held accountable? You must understand the concept of Divine Decree better. Al-Qadar (Divine Decree) comprises four components. The first component is the belief that God is All-Knowledgeable. His Knowledge encompasses all things. The Almighty's foreknowledge is infallible and complete.

"And with Him are the keys of the unseen; none knows them except Him. And He knows what is on the land and in the sea. Not a leaf falls but that He knows it. And no grain is there within the darknesses of the earth and no moist or dry thing but that it is written in a clear record" (Quran 6:59)

The second component of Divine Decree is the belief that Allah has recorded all happenings, everything from the beginning of time to the Day of Judgment, in a Tablet He has kept an account known as the *Lawh Al-Mahfooth (the Preserved Tablet)*. Each person's lifespan, substance, deeds, happiness, sorrows, and more are written and recorded on this Tablet. In fact, according to a narration of Prophet Muhammad PBUH, Allah, the Glorious, recorded the measurements of all matters regarding His creation fifty thousand years before He created the heavens and the earth.

"Do you not know that Allah knows what is in the Heaven and Earth? Indeed, that is in a Record. Indeed that, for Allah, is easy" (Quran 22:70)

The third component of Divine Decree is the belief that nothing can occur without the Will and Power of Allah, whether the event stems from the action of the Almighty or the actions of humanity. Nothing occurs haphazardly or by accident; the Almighty has decreed everything.

Muslims acknowledge that anything that has happened could not have been avoided or prevented--no one can avoid an occurrence unless God has willed it. By contrast, whatever has not reached, attained, or afflicted a person, was not meant to touch or afflict that person by God's will. Our Prophet PBUH narrated, *"Know if all of humanity gathered to harm you, they could not harm you unless Allah had decreed. The Pen has been lifted, and the pages have dried."*

The fourth and last component of Divine Decree is the belief that Allah is the Creator and Originator of all things.

"...and has created each thing and determined it with precise determination" (Quran 25:2)

If you question why you are held responsible for the choices and actions you make if God decreed all of them before your birth, you must realize that whatever was written about you was written only because you will make those choices on your own. You would not be making your choices in life because they were written beforehand. They were written beforehand because God can foretell the future, and He decided to write everything that will happen until the day of Judgement on a tablet. But because God wrote all that will occur in your life in a tablet doesn't mean that God determined or dictated the choices and actions you will take and that these decisions are preordained for you against your will. God wrote all your actions because you will commit them; you did not commit them before God wrote them. Everyone has free will to make whatever choice they want.

This concept may be difficult for some to grasp, and some may find its truth to be a contradiction to everything that has been said previously, but it is not, in fact, a contradiction. To summarize, what God wrote down in the beginning, was written because you ultimately make these choices on your own. You will not make your choices because they were written; they were written because you will make those choices.

The fact that God has written down all things does not change the truth that humans have the free will to choose their course of action. Just because each person's choices are known to God beforehand, because He is All-Knowing, doesn't mean that one will not be held accountable

17

for their decisions and actions on the Day of Judgment. God's Knowledge of the future does not allow humans free agency to do as they wish. God forces nothing upon anyone. God will hold no one accountable for things out of their control or for something they cannot do. Allah is All-Just and All-Wise; He tests humanity according to their strength and what their soul can bear. Muslims acknowledge that whatever difficulty they face is surmountable and that they can resolve it.

"God does not burden any human being
with more than he is well able to bear" (Quran 2:286)

Muslims acknowledge that whatever befalls them is by God's Will and Plan, whether they understand or accept this. Muslims place their trust and reliance on God, as God brims with Wisdom in all matters. Muslims affirm that God is All-Loving and loves His servants more than even their parents do. Muslims affirm that whatever God does holds a good motive, so believers always assume the goodness of life and do not lose faith.

Divine Decree never will be fully understood and comprehended by humans, as the concept deals with the essence of God's Power and Will beyond that which our finite minds can comprehend.

Muslims benefit from learning, believing, and understanding Divine Decree in several ways. Amongst its benefits is the peace of mind and contentment of the heart that Muslims will attain if they acknowledge that nothing happens without a purpose. Muslims are confident that whatever has afflicted them could not have escaped them, and whatever missed them could not have reached them. God is in complete control of all happenings and events and predestines all. This recognition enables a believer to endure difficulties and hardships. Muslims do not grieve over what could have happened if things had taken a different course. Muslims do not worry about the future because they know that tomorrow's events are written and predetermined.

The act of learning and believing in the Divine Decree increases and enhances one's belief and trust in God. One's reliance on God increases the likelihood of performing good deeds increases. Faith in Divine Decree decreases pride and arrogance in one's deeds, as believers acknowledge that their intelligence and actions did not emanate from them; God is the source of all that comes their way. Belief in Divine Decree makes people refrain from fear, inspiring bravery as they acknowledge that no one can inflict harm on them without God's permission and the Will of God. Without a strong belief in God, life would not be worth living.

Does Islam Believe in Evolution?

In general, Muslims accept the theory of evolution-- there are many types of evolution Muslims have no issue affirming. Muslims generally have no problems with the concept of microevolution. Muslims have no issues affirming the evolution of animals over time, adapting to their environment, and developing an immunity to negotiate their environment. For example, the beaks of an animal can evolve to assume different shapes and sizes to access food on a particular island better, or an animal can develop thicker skin over the years to survive better in their habitat. This process displays the power and intelligence of the Creator of all, God the Almighty. Muslims also do not have an issue believing that all animals might have come from the same origin animal because this belief doesn't go against the Holy Quran and the sayings of Prophet Muhammad PBUH. A name of Allah, after all, is Al-Bari, which means the Evolver, the giver of forms.

On the other hand, Muslims cannot accept Darwinian evolution or human evolution, where human beings evolved from pre-human ancestors, as it goes against the Holy Quran. We believe everything stated in the Holy Quran because we have good reasons to believe that the entire text came from our Creator. The Holy Quran explicitly states that God fashioned Adam with his own two hands. God created Adam as a fully formed man, not a baby. He created Adam PBUH from a pool of mud with components of clay, soil, Earth, and water. Then God breathed life into him. Then God taught him the name of all things. Then he brought down Prophet Adam PBUH to this Earth. From Adam and Eve came multitudes of men and women. Adam was born miraculously without the intervention or presence of a father or a mother. Human beings were created separately from animals and other creations.

"Recall when your Lord said to the angels, "I will create a human being out of clay from an altered black mud" (Quran 15:28)

"O humanity! Be mindful of your Lord Who created you from a single soul, and from it He created its mate, and through both He spread countless men and women..." (Quran 4:1)

It's imperative to note that the miraculous creation of Adam PBUH cannot be confirmed or rejected by science, nor can science disprove the existence of God. Since science is restricted to providing natural explanations explaining how things work, it cannot explain who created things and why. We need Revelation and religion to provide these explanations. Everything around us is living evidence of an intelligent designer behind it. The origin of our universe has a cause, and we know that chaos cannot create such an intelligently designed system. However, the scientific method cannot indicate the cause of the creation of the universe and why it was created since science looks only at nature—that is, what we can observe, touch, see, and smell--and tries to find natural explanations, excluding anything outside of nature. As for things outside of the natural world, science has no way of dealing with them. Science doesn't take into account the metaphysical realm, the unseen world, so science cannot include explanations not based on nature, like pointing to the Divine as the cause of the universe's inception.

"And Allah has created from water every living creature. Some of them crawl on their bellies, some walk on two legs, and some walk on four. Allah creates whatever He wills. Surely Allah is Most Capable of everything" (Quran 24:45)

Science and religion can coexist. Aside from Darwin's theory of evolution, the teachings of Islam do not necessarily conflict with scientific explanations of the natural world. Muslims understand that the process of natural selection and other forms of evolution do not occur of their own accord. Instead, they are simply evidence of the existence of an intelligent designer and fashioner behind them, one who controls everything and wills everything to occur. He is our Creator.

No other creation of God compares to the creation of human beings, as human beings have intellect, culture, and other assets that differentiate them from other creations. Simply because humans share some DNA with chimpanzees doesn't mean humans evolved from apes. Humans also share some similar DNA to bananas, but that doesn't mean humans share a common ancestor with fruit.

Muslims have no problem believing other creations exist or have existed in the past, which we may have never known about. Simply because Muslims believe that Prophet Adam PBUH was the first human that ever lived doesn't necessarily mean that no two-legged creations of God walked upright before the creation of Adam PBUH. The Holy Quran is silent about whether there were predecessors of Adam PBUH in that regard. If fossil records are discovered depicting human-like upright bipedal apes with the ability to walk with two legs, large brains, and use tools, a belief in such animals will not go against the Holy Quran or Sunnah. Still, one thing is for sure; these creatures would not be the forefathers of Prophet Adam PBUH, as that belief would certainly go against the Holy Quran and Sunnah.

"...And He creates that which you do not know." (Quran 16:8)

What is the Concept of Hell?
Can Hell be Justified?

Why Did God Create Hell, Knowing that Some People Will Be Condemned?

W e'll go over the concept of Hell in some detail before discussing why God would create Hell, knowing that some people will be condemned. Life is a test, with the test ending at death. Every atom of good and evil that one performs in their lifetime is recorded in their book of deeds, a book to be presented on the Day of Judgment--when every soul will be held accountable for their actions. While in the grave, the deceased souls that deserve to go to Hell will experience suffering, whereas those bound for Paradise will experience peace while awaiting the Day of Resurrection.

God is the Arbitrator who will judge, recompense, reward, or punish His creation. When the hour comes, God will raise every deceased person, including the Jinn (supernatural creatures), to judge them according to their deeds in life. Whereas God is Most-Forgiving, He is also Just. If one's good deeds outweigh their bad deeds, they will enter Paradise and join the successful. By contrast, the individuals whose bad deeds outweigh their good deeds will suffer Hellfire. Standing among Islam's most fundamental aspects dictates that life's purpose is to save oneself from the punishment of Hellfire and enter Paradise eternally.

"Every soul will taste death, and you will only be given your full compensation on the Day of Resurrection. So he who is drawn away from the Fire and admitted to Paradise has attained his desire. And what is the life of this world except for the enjoyment of delusion" (Quran 3:185)

Believing and accepting the reality of the Last Day, Judgment Day, Paradise, and Hellfire is a component of the Six Pillars of Iman (Faith) that every Muslim must believe and accept. Many references to Hellfire are listed throughout the Holy Quran and in the sayings of the Prophet Muhammad PBUH.

The finite human mind cannot imagine the pain, horrors, anguish, hardship, humiliation, restlessness, and all forms of punishment of Hellfire. Not everyone lingering in Hell will suffer in the same manner. Those in Hellfire will suffer tremendously, both physically and spiritually. The gravity of one's sins will distinguish and dictate the severity of the suffering.

Allah, the Exalted, prepares and reserves Hellfire for those who do not believe in Him, believe in gods other than Allah, rebel against God's Religion and Laws, and reject God's Message and Messengers. Hellfire is for sinners, criminals, murderers, tyrants, hypocrites, the proud and the arrogant, stubborn, unjust, and evil people.

"Do they not know that whoever opposes Allah and His Messenger - that for him is the Fire of Hell, wherein he will abide eternally? That is the great disgrace" (Quran 9:63)

Islam states that salvation is based on faith in Allah, His Messenger, good deeds, and God's Mercy. It is the nature of God to treat no one unjustly or unfairly. As part of the Justice of God, the Almighty, He punishes no one person or no group of people unless and until He has sent them a messenger relaying his Message.

"...And never would We punish until We sent a messenger"
(Quran 17:15)

Among the most severe cause of suffering that unbelievers and evildoers will face on the Day of Judgment is the realization that they did not follow God's Message nor His Guidance and have failed in life, thus earning God's Wrath. Many dwellers of Hellfire will instantly regret the choices they have made in their lives and beg for another chance. The Quran states:

And those who followed would say: 'If only We had one more chance, we would clear ourselves of them, as they have cleared themselves of us' Thus, will Allah show them the fruits of their deeds as nothing but regrets. Nor will there be a way for them out of the Fire" (Quran 2:167)

The Holy Quran shares a dialogue that will take place between the dwellers of Hellfire and the Angel Gatekeeper of Hell on the Day of Judgment.

"It almost explodes in rage. Whenever a group is thrown into it, its keepers will ask them, 'Did there not come to you a warner?' They will reply: 'Yes indeed; a Warner did come to us, but we rejected him and said, 'Allah never sent down any Message: You are but lost in a great delusion!' 'And they will add: 'Had we but listened to those warnings, or at least used our own reason, we would not now be among those who are destined for the blazing flame!' They will then confess their sins: but far will be Forgiveness from the Companions of the Blazing Fire!"
(Quran 67:8-10)

However, no matter how sinners beg for forgiveness, it will be too late to receive this boon. The intensity of the Fire will be so terrifying that people will disown the closest and most beloved in their lives on the Day of Judgment and flee from them on this great Day.

"But when there comes the Deafening Blast. On the Day a man will flee from his brother. And his mother and his father. And his wife and his children. For every man, that Day, will be a matter adequate for him." (Quran 33-37)

Man will surrender all he holds dear to save himself from Hellfire.

They will be shown each other. The criminal will wish he could be ransomed from the punishment of that Day by his children. And his wife and his brother. And his nearest kindred who shelter him. And whoever is on Earth entirely so then it could save him" (Quran 70:14)

A quick flash of Hellfire will cause a person to forget in an instant all of the pleasures they enjoyed in their lifetime. Our Prophet PBUH narrated: *One of the people of Hell who found the most pleasure in the life of this world will be brought forth on the Day of Resurrection and dipped into the Fire of Hell. Then he will be asked, 'O son of Adam, have you ever seen anything good?' Have you ever enjoyed any pleasure?' He will say, 'No, by God, O Lord.'* (Sahih Muslim)

Whereas a minority of Islamic scholars state that people will not burn in Hellfire eternally, most express the notion that the polytheist and unbelievers will reside in Hellfire forever. Hellfire is eternal for the many that enter this dreaded realm.

"Indeed, Allah has cursed the disbelievers and prepared for them a Blaze. Abiding therein forever, they will not find a protector or a helper" (Quran 33:64-65)

God, the Almighty, created Hellfire and Paradise before humanity. Hellfire is black and as dark as night. Hell knows such depths that if one were to drop a stone into this realm, seventy years would pass before that stone hit bottom.

Hellfire holds various levels of severity and punishment according to the extent of disbelief and the severity of sins suffered by those punished. The lower the level of the Fire, the greater the intensity and punishment one suffers. Our Prophet PBUH narrated that the lightest punishment of Hellfire would involve placing one's feet on a smoldering ember, and his brains would boil as a result of this treatment. The most severe punishment in Hellfire will be assigned to the hypocrites, as God states in His Book:

"Indeed, the hypocrites will be in the lowest depths of the Fire - and never will you find for them a helper" (Quran 4:145)

Hellfire has Seven Gates through which new inhabitants will enter. Each gate is reserved for a specific group or category of sinners, containing different varieties of torture and punishments. The distance between each gate is equal to the length of seventy years. Before the inhabitants of Hell enter, they will stand before the gate, feeling the heat in terror. They will be shoved and piled through the first gate until it fills; then, the rest will be stacked and pushed into the second gate until it too loads to capacity, and so on.

Hellfire is staffed by nineteen Angels, led by the chief keeper of Hellfire named *Angel Malik,* who never has smiled since the time of his creation. Angel Malik and the Angels of Hellfire are severe, harsh, and stern and never disobey God's commandments.

After the inhabitants of Hellfire enter this realm, the gates will be shut with no hope of escape for dwellers. They will beg and plead to Angel Malik to release them, and he will respond, "*Be quiet, surely; you shall abide forever!*" The Angels of Hellfire bear whips made of iron to whip the inhabitants within. The dwellers of Hellfire will take animosity and hate toward other inhabitants of Hellfire.

"Indeed, the criminals will be in the punishment of Hell, abiding eternally. The torment will not be lightened for them, and they will be plunged into destruction with deep regrets, sorrows and in despair therein. And We did not wrong them, but it was they who were the wrongdoers. And they will call, 'O Malik, let your Lord put an end to us!' He will say, 'Indeed, you will remain. We had certainly brought you the truth, but most of you, to the truth, were averse.' (Quran 43:-74-78)

In regards to those believers who practiced Tawheed (monotheism) and who believed in the Prophet sent to them from God but lived a sinful life, they will be punished in Hellfire for a length commensurate with the level of their sins. Some will be taken from Hellfire due to the Prophets' intercession, some by righteous individuals' intercession, and some will be released solely by the Mercy of God, the Most Merciful. After they are freed, eventually, they are sent to Paradise.

The Fire that exists and burns in our world is 1/70th of the severity and intensity of Hellfire that burns in the Hereafter. The Fire kindled by the Almighty will burn the skin of its inhabitants; every time their skin gets roasted, it will melt to their feet, and God the Almighty will replace this burnt skin with a new one to be burnt yet again. The process will repeat to allow for more punishment. Other forms of punishment include the application of excessively heated burring oil, which will be poured onto their heads to melt away and liquefy their internal organs. The inhabitants of Hellfire will wear chains and shackles, which will be tied around their necks and feet.

"Indeed, We have prepared for the disbelievers chains and shackles and a blaze" (Quran 76:4)

Those who ask why a beneficent God would create Hellfire should realize that this question is irrelevant in determining whether God exists. The fact that God created Hellfire does not negate His existence. And why are you attempting to rationalize something you do not believe in the first place? Or do you believe deep inside and struggle to submit to your Creator?

God does not need your permission to create or throw you into Hellfire. The more important question to consider is what you are doing to save yourself from Hellfire. Are you actively trying to find God, the truth of His religion, while trying to obey Him? Are you verifying that your beliefs are true? Are you pondering Islam and the concept of God in Islam, reflecting on whether it makes sense to you?

**"He cannot be questioned about what He does,
but they will all be questioned" (Quran 21:23)**

God the Almighty, the Most Merciful and the Most Compassionate, did not create Hellfire for the joy of throwing people into it, nor does he want to do so. God asks a rhetorical question in the Holy Quran, stating:

**"What can Allah gain by your punishment if you are grateful and believe? And ever is Allah Appreciative and Knowing"
(Quran 4:147)**

God will gain nothing from punishing anyone and seeks every good reason not to condemn. God states in the Holy Quran that He created humanity and Jinn to worship Him, glorify Him, and exalt Him, as He is the Only One worthy of worship. He states in another verse that from his end, He created humanity to show them His Mercy:

**"Except whom your Lord has given mercy,
and for that He created them...." (Quran 11:119)**

One must realize that God is All-knowing, All-Wise, Most-Merciful, and Just. If God tells us He completed an action, we cannot question as to why He did it, nor if it is appropriate to do. We are not in a place to assume that the act of God throwing certain people into Hellfire is unjust and wrong when the action extends beyond our limited human scope.

The believer must realize that he is a slave and God is his Master. One cannot question Him or His authority, nor do they have any right to do so. A Master can be just and kind or unjust and unkind. Allah, the Exalted, is a Merciful Master. If one accepts that they are Allah's slave and submits to Him fully, they will find God is the most Beneficent and Merciful. Only when one surrenders to His Master does one find that his life is easier and better.

Why would God want to punish an individual when He created them with love and mercy in the first place? God wants to warn his servants about Hell now, so they can fix themselves and avoid it to the best of their ability. It is best to be informed about Hellfire now and recognize its severity, harshness, and gruesome punishment rather than to come across it unprepared in the Hereafter. That is Mercy, as God the Almighty could have chosen not to warn one of the consequences of one's actions. While God is Most-Merciful, He is also All-Just. He states in the Quran:

**"Indeed, Allah does not do injustice,
even as much as an atom's weight..." (Quran 4:40)**

One needs to note that God is Most Merciful. Muslims do not attest that God is All-Merciful, as Christians do. An All-Merciful God would show mercy to everyone unconditionally, even though those who don't deserve it, such as serial killers and rapists. God is Most Merciful and All-Just and shows Mercy to those who deserve it. If God showered mercy on everyone unconditionally and forgave everyone for every sin, he would not be serving justice to victims oppressed by the people who wronged them.

God is also All-Just. Hence, evildoers and sinners must be held accountable for their actions. If one commits murder or oppresses another individual, God may punish that person to serve justice to the one killed or oppressed—or to serve justice to the victim's family members. God states that every soul shall receive total compensation for their good and evil deeds on the Day of Judgment.

God is Righteous and Fair. If He didn't punish evil, He would allow that evil to exist without consequences, encouraging people to oppress and commit evil, spreading corruption even further. The fear of punishment prevents people from committing evil. Since God cannot permit this evil to transpire, His justice requires that a proper punishment be incurred and executed for evil sins. God also states that he will forgive any soul that repents from their sin, as He is Extremely Forgiving and Extremely Loving. Although Allah is not answerable to anyone, He has promised to be Just and Fair to everyone.

Humans are motivated by reward and punishment. Some need consequences or punishment to empower them to stop their sinning. Hellfire is a deterrent for those who disbelieve, disobey God, and commit evil. Hellfire exists for those who need serious deterrents to turn them from evil, and Paradise is there to motivate those who need a reward to do good. What better than Paradise as a reward for those who believe in God and obey Him?

Those who ask why God throws "good people" into Hellfire need to realize that they cannot fully judge the difference between good deeds and bad deeds, and they cannot classify what constitutes a "good person" from a "bad person." One might appear to be good, doing some good deeds, but at the same time might mistreat their parents at home, or are perhaps too stubborn to submit, worship, and obey their Creator despite recognizing God's existence and the truth--thus making them a bad person. No one on the Day of Judgment would feel they had been meted injustice, whether they go to Paradise or Hell. Only God can make such a judgment; you and I cannot, so we should make no assumptions without seeing the complete picture, without possessing the full knowledge that God has.

Only those who deserve to be thrown into Hellfire will be condemned; those who disbelieved and disobeyed God and wasted time despite having time on Earth to ponder and repent for their actions. God will throw no one into Hellfire unless they have been given a fair opportunity to gain Paradise. God tells us that we agreed through our covenant with Him to take a test of life on Earth through the free will that gives us a chance to earn Paradise - or Hellfire if we disbelieve and disobey.

It would have been unjust for God to create humans and throw them into Hellfire without testing them in this world. So, God tests everyone on this Earth for some time before entering Paradise or Hellfire. God says in the Holy Book that those who will be thrown into Hellfire will accept God's judgment but still beg for another chance to live on Earth and live righteously; however, God states that if He did send them back to this world, they would have forgotten and chosen the path of evil once again, with the same destiny awaiting them afterward.

Certain individuals want to blame God for Hell because they do not want to fix their acts, face reality, or be held accountable for their actions. It's essential to realize that whether you believe, like, and accept God and Hellfire or not, it will not change the fact that God and Hellfire do exist— just as if you dislike or do not believe in the presence of heavy traffic outside on the roads, it wouldn't mean that you won't encounter traffic when you go outside to drive.

"O, you who have believed, protect yourselves and your families from a Fire whose fuel is people and stones...." (Quran 66:6)

Could Prophet Muhammad PBUH have Copied its Text from Another Source? Could the Holy Quran Be Inspired by Satan?

The Holy Quran is standing proof of the truthfulness of Islam. Anyone who thoroughly examines the text of the Holy Quran will conclude that no one, including the Prophet Muhammad PBUH, could have authored this Book, as no human being could produce anything like it. Thus, the text could come only from God, the Almighty, the All-Wise.

The Holy Quran stands as the eternal miracle of the Prophet Muhamad PBUH, providing the truthfulness and very basis of his Prophethood. Past prophets performed miracles to prove their own Prophethood, but the manifestations of all of these miracles ended with their deaths, as they were Prophets who served their people only. Since Prophet Muhammad, PBUH, is the last Prophet and is meant to be followed until the end of time, the manifestation of his miracle needs to last until this time, so the people who live after him can see his miracle and believe in his Prophethood. Therefore, the Holy Quran remains preserved and exists today--just as it did more than 1400 years ago.

For many reasons, Prophet Muhammad PBUH could not have been the earthly author of the Holy Quran. Let us now examine some clear proof of this edict. First, Prophet Muhammad PBUH did not know how to read or write, nor did he attend any schools or travel outside the Arabian Peninsula. So, the Holy Quran was sent down to an unlettered Prophet who did not read, write, or calculate. He had no education or communication skills to demonstrate to the people that he could not have authored the Holy Text.

Prophet Muhammad PBUH would not have possessed the ability to compose a Book that became the masterpiece of the Arabic language. The Holy Quran is inimitable in style, form, and spiritual impact; it has a unique rhythm, tone, rhyme, and genre like no other book. The Holy Quran contains the highest possible standard of linguistics and rhetoric in its speech, to the extent that it would be impossible for a human or group of humans to produce.

Prophet Muhammad PBUH was not known to compose poetry, nor did he like it. If Prophet Muhamad PBUH were lying about his illiteracy, his enemies would have known—this owing to the fact that Prophet Muhammad PBUH grew up in the same city, Mecca, as many of his enemies.

"You, O Prophet, could not read any writing even before this revelation, nor could you write at all. Otherwise, the people of falsehood would have been suspicious" (Quran 29:48)

The question remains, how could Prophet Muhammad PBUH have been the author of the Holy Quran when he lived in the midst of the Arabian desert with no teachers or libraries? After all, the Arabic Peninsula existed as a backward, antiquated nation then? The Holy Quran references a variety of forward-thinking facts, resources of knowledge, and various sciences that people could not have known at the time and place in which the Prophet Muhammad PBUH and his companions existed.

The Holy Quran contains knowledge, guidance, and helpful information to explain complicated matters about inheritance, civil law, criminal law, history, finance, business, tax law, military law, embryology, labor law, real estate law, family law, dietary laws, psychology, raising children, marriage, worship, oceanography, biography, universe, physics, medicine, astronomy, and more. It presents this information using simple speech and imagery in Arabic, with no errors or contradicting principles. Moreover, the Holy Quran uses terminology and descriptions at an advanced level beyond what a 7th-century person living in the desert would know.

Early biographical reports state that Prophet Muhammad PBUH was known in his community as truthful and trustworthy due to his early reputation for displaying these qualities. He never was accused of telling a solitary lie.

The Holy Quran is the greatest miracle of God and contains a recounting of thousands of miracles to prove its Godly origins. It is a lofty statement for any book to claim to contain the official word of God. Without clear evidence or with one contradiction found within the Book, the apparent Word of God would be proven false. Yet the Holy Quran does not contain any contradictions, nor is any information confirmed to be incorrect. Also disproving the idea that this Book could not have come from Prophet Muhammad PBUH, or any person or group of people for that matter is the fact that the Holy Quran contains hundreds of scientific facts later confirmed to be accurate years after the Book was revealed, proving its Divine origin. This book came from a higher power.

The Holy Quran was revealed to the Prophet Muhammad PBUH in the 7th century to an illiterate man living in the desert, at a time when no telescopes, microscopes, or anything resembling the symbols of advanced modern technology existed. However, as popular faith in Islam continued to grow century after century, humanity evolved into the age of modern science. In this era, many scientific discoveries have occurred to confirm certain verses of the Holy Quran.

The Holy Quran, for example, states every living thing is made from water. It was not until years after its publication, after the invention of the microscope, that scientists confirmed this fact, that every living thing consists primarily of water. Also notable is the fact that The Holy Quran addresses the evolution of the human embryo in the mother's womb in chronological order. And in a time where many humans initially thought that the world was flat, the Holy Quran references the Earth as being shaped like an ostrich egg, which is geo-spherical.

Whereas people initially believed that the Moon casts its own light, the Holy Quran references the fact that the Moon's light is not natural to this celestial being, but instead takes the form of reflected light—a point scientists have confirmed to be accurate. The Bible, on the other hand, relayed the original, mistaken perception. This is because the Bible contains words of men, and not God.

The Holy Quran references the idea that God made mountains in the form of pegs, much like those objects that hold up tents. Mountains stand tall to provide the Earth's stability, preventing the planet from shaking--much like pegs stand to offer stability to a tent. Like tent pegs, mountains bear deep roots embedded in the Earth. The Holy Quran also contains a dialogue of a queen ant who warns her community against the dangers of being stepped on; and we now know that the animals whose life cycles most closely resemble our own are none other than ants. They routinely meet and communicate in their nests, with the Queen Ants issuing instructions.

Here I have outlined only a few of the many scientific miracles presented in the Holy Quran. Conduct an internet search to learn about many others that exist. How could an illiterate man living in the desert possess such advanced knowledge at the historical time in which he lived unless this knowledge came from above?

The intricate detailing of linguistic and scientific miracles are not the only evidence presented in the Holy Quran that disproves Prophet

Muhammad PBUH's authorship, as the book also contains many prophecies that have since come true. In addition, the Holy Quran provides many predictions related to future events. In truth, all these Quranic predictions manifested as predicated.

Among the many accurate futuristic predictions in the Quran is the bold claim that the Byzantine Empire would reign victorious over the Persian Empire. The Holy Quran stated that the body of the Pharaoh who lived in the time of Prophet Moses PBUH would be preserved as a sign for those who came after him. His body was discovered in 1898 and is now kept in a museum. In the early '70s, his corpse was examined. An examination conducted through an investigation of his mummy concluded that he had died from water infiltration into his lung, providing conclusive proof of a drowning death. The examination also revealed that he lived at the time of the Prophet Moses PBUH. The Holy Quran predicted and promised that Muslims would re-enter the Sacred House of Allah, Mecca, victoriously in a state of security. This later came true in the eighth year of the Hijrah.

Many other prophecies fill the Holy Quran; for instance, God's claim that He would safeguard and protect his final Book to humanity, the Holy Quran, from human-made alterations or any form of corruption. Nevertheless, the Holy Quran remains the same way it was revealed, letter by letter.

The Holy Quran also contains God's claim that He rendered the text easy to memorize. Today, millions of people have memorized the entire Book successfully, which includes more than 600 pages, regardless of their ethnicity and language. No other scripture or book on Earth is equally easy to memorize.

The Holy Quran prophesizes future happenings and tells many stories of past events, nations, and prophets, such as the stories of Prophet Joseph, Moses, and Jesus, peace be upon them. The Prophet Muhammad PBUH lived in the middle of the desert with not a library in

37

sight, as the Arabic Peninsula was a backward, antiquated nation at the time. He was unlettered and grew up among illiterate idol worshippers without knowledge of the previous Scriptures. He had no way of reading or conjuring these stories shared in the Holy Quan.

"That is from the news of the unseen which We reveal to you, [O Muhammad]. You knew it not, neither you nor your people, before this. So be patient; indeed, the best outcome is for the righteous" (Quran 11:49)

The idea that Prophet Muhammad PBUH copied stories from the Old and New Testament is not a logical one; because if he did indeed replicate the stories from these sources, then he would have copied those passages of the Bible that were accurate, as well as the parts that were not accurate. The Bible contains thousands of errors and contradictions, but you don't see any of those errors reflected in the pages of the Holy Quran. In addition, Prophet Muhammad PBUH lacked direct access to the previous books. The Old Testament in Arabic did not arrive in the Arabian Peninsula until two hundred years after the departure of Prophet Muhammad PBUH, and the Arabic New Testament did not arrive until a thousand years afterward.

For those who think that the Prophet Muhammad PBUH might have fabricated his Prophethood for worldly gain, it is imperative to realize that the Prophet Muhammad PBUH, his companions, and his family underwent many years of persecution, hardship, boycott, exile, and lost kinship because they believed in and spread the message of God - just like the past Prophets of God and their followers. Prophet Muhammad PBUH was denied food, had dirt thrown upon him and was pelted with stones because he was spreading the word of God. Still, he remained persistent even while witnessing the prosecution and torture of his family and friends. The Prophets of God did not come down in search of worldly gain. They wanted only to spread the Word of God, causing them great hardship, and material gain was never their objective--nor did they accept it.

Prophet Muhammad PBUH did not compose the Holy Quran for riches, as he was married to the wealthiest woman in Mecca. Prophet Muhammad PBUH lived a simple, humble, and frugal life, sitting and sleeping on a mat on the floor, mending his clothes, and he died without money because he did not pursue or care for the materialistic lifestyle.

Prophet Muhammad PBUH was offered exalted leadership roles and wealth to halt his spread of the Message of God, but he refused because he didn't care for power or government leadership.

Contrary to what some believe, Prophet Muhammad PBUH did not write the Holy Quran to attempt to unite the Arabs. The Holy Quran does not contain any Verses that talk about uniting the Arabs, and only conveys the concept of uniting the Muslim nation of all races.

It's not reasonable to believe that Prophet Muhammad PBUH wrote the Holy Quran, when it contains Verses that admonish Prophet Muhammad PBUH. Why would Prophet Muhmmad PBUH write a Book where he admonished himself, undermining his position of authority? The Holy Quran states about Prophet Muhammad PBUH:

"He frowned and turned his attention away simply because the blind man came to him interrupting. You never know, O Prophet, perhaps he may be purified, or he may be mindful, benefitting from the remainder" (Quran 80:1-4)

"It is not fit for a prophet that he should take captives until he has thoroughly subdued the land. You believers settled with the fleeting gains of this world, while Allah's aim for you is the Hereafter. Allah is Almighty, All-Wise" (Quran 8:67)

"...And you feared the people, while Allah has more right that you fear Him..." (Quran 33:37)

"O Prophet! Why do you prohibit yourself from what Allah has made lawful to you, seeking to please your wives? And Allah is All-Forgiving, Most Merciful" (Quran 66:1)

There Holy Quran has a Verse where Allah commands Prophet Muhammad PBUH to communicate to his followers that he (Prophet Muhammad PBUH) only follows what is revealed to him. He was letting his followers know that the commands were coming from God and not from himself and that he was only a warner.

"Say, "I am not the first messenger ever sent, nor do I know what will happen to me or you. I only follow what is revealed to me. And I am only sent with a clear warning" (Quran 46:9)

At the age of approximately sixty, Prophet Muhammad PBUH had a son whom he named Abraham. Unfortunately, Abraham became ill and passed away. Prophet Muhammad PBUH was in pain, crying about the passing of his son. At that time, the Sun eclipsed - a full solar eclipse in which the Moon passed between the Sun and Earth, completely blocking the face of the Sun in the daytime while causing the Sky to darken as if it were dawn or dusk.

Rumors started to spread around Medina that even the Sky was suffused with sadness regarding the death of the Prophet's son, Abraham. When Prophet Muhammad PBUH buried his son, he called the people to the Mosque. They prayed, after which Prophet Muhammad PBH stood up and stated to his people: "Verily, the Sun and the Moon are signs of Allah's existence; they do not eclipse on account of the death or birth of anyone."

This is a powerful demonstration that Prophet Muhammad PBUH was a true prophet. If he or anyone was truly a false prophet, and this happened to him, they would have taken advantage of the moment and not hastened to correct the rumors. However, since he was indeed the true Prophet of God, he had to speak the truth and tell people that the eclipse played no role in the death of his son.

Satan is the sworn enemy of humanity, who has been granted respite until the Day of Judgment. He tries to tempt human beings to sin, glamorize sin, and deceive humanity into deterring them from remembrance and obedience to God. Those who think Satan authored the Holy Quran or that Prophet Muhammad PBUH was inspired to write it by Satan probably have never read it. This is simply an absurd claim for many reasons.

The Holy Quran arrived in the Arabian Peninsula when the people of Mecca were devoted to idol worship. The period at the time spawned ignorance, foolishness, and misguidance. The Holy Quran and Prophet Muhammad PBUH came down, telling the wayward people to leave their idol worship and worship the One True God, thus empowering them to avoid hellfire and enter Paradise.

Why would Satan write a Book or inspire Prophet Muhammad PBUH to call upon idol worshippers to stop worshipping false idols and worship the One God? It would be highly counterproductive to do so. Idol worshipping carves the path to Hell and worshipping the One true God is the path to Paradise. Satan would not want humanity to depart the path of Hell and take instead the path of Paradise.

A Verse in the Holy Quan tells us to seek refuge in Allah from Satan, the accursed before we start reading the Holy Quran. The Holy Quran warns us that Satan is our clear enemy and advises us not to follow in his footsteps; whoever does so enjoins immortality and wrongdoing. The Holy Quran portrays Satan as an arrogant, racist, disobedient, and ungrateful liar. Why would Satan curse himself and command people to turn away from him, worshipping God instead?

The Holy Quran is filled with Verses commanding people to be good and fair, to help the poor, to pray and fast, and to perform other good acts. The Holy Quran commands people to speak kindly, politely, graciously, fairly, with justice, and without lying. The Holy Quran forbids adultery, drinking alcohol, gambling, violence, usury, stealing, dishonesty, murder, and many other illicit acts Satan tempts humanity to commit. So why would Satan command society to do good and prohibit them from doing what is not good?

The Holy Quran challenges anyone who doubts the Book's Divine origins to produce another sacred text equal in merit, a text that matches its eloquence, power, style, and language and is free from error and contradictions. Any document that claims to include the Word of God bears a heavy burden. Without clear evidence or with the presence of even one contradiction within the Book, the apparent Word of God would be proven false.

The Holy Quran is devoid of contradictions and contains no information confirmed to be incorrect, even though the whole text was not revealed at once. Instead, it was revealed orally over a twenty-three-year period piece by piece, with each passage often coming down in the wake of a current event happening in the time of Prophet Muhammad PBUH and his early companions, without the benefit of an editorial process to amend its content.

Allah made it clear that no one will ever be able to produce anything comparable to the Holy Quran—not even one chapter like it—thus affirming another prophecy of the Holy Quran. This challenge stands unchallenged, with no one writing a text comparable to the Holy Quran. Not even during the time of the Prophet PBUH, when Arabs emerged as masters of the Arabic language, according to historians and linguists.

"And if you are in doubt about what We have sent down upon Our Servant [Muhammad], then produce a Surah (Chapter) the like thereof and call upon your witnesses other than Allah, if you should be truthful" (Quran 2:23)

What fallible human, or group of humans for that matter, would write a book of more than 600 pages and challenge humanity to find contradictions or discrepancies within its pages? Everything in the Holy Quran is true, with no evidence of contradictions or falseness. It will remain in perfect form for eternity because it is the Word of God, who is perfect and makes no mistakes. If this Book were from Prophet Muhammad PBUH, a group of people, or Satan, it would contain mistakes, errors, and contradictions—this is owing to the fact that everyone except God is fallible. In comparison, the Bible is filled with falsehoods and contradictions, making it clear that its text has been tampered with by human hands and is not the word of God.

"Then do they not reflect upon the Quran? If it had been from any other than Allah, they would have found within it much contradiction" (Quran 4:82)

Why Did the Caliph Uthman Burn Different Versions of the Quran?

Prophet Muhammad PBUH received the text of the Holy Quran from Angel Gabriel, who, in turn, received it directly from God. The Holy Quran was not revealed to Prophet Muhammad PBUH at one time, nor were they revealed to him in order. Instead, the Verses of the Holy Quran were revealed to Prophet Muhammad PBUH over the course of 23 years and often would be delivered in the wake of a current event happening in the time of Prophet Muhammad PBUH and his early Muslim companions.

Angel Gabriel instructed Prophet Muhammad PBUH where Verses and Chapters belonged so that he could sequence the Holy Quran correctly. Prophet Muhammad PBUH instructed scribes to write verbatim as he dictated them orally. The scribes of the Prophet PBUH would write the Verses of the Holy Quran as dictated on whatever surface they had available, whether it took the form of leather, white stones, bones, animal skin, pieces of bark, etc. His main scribe was named Zaid bin Thabit R.A.

Whereas Quranic Verses were composed in fragments, the Holy Quran was compiled into a Book--one developed within two years after the passing of the Prophet PBUH when his major companions were still alive. During a battle, many Quranic memorizers were killed, so the scribe of Prophet Muhammad PBUH, Zaid bin Thabit, was asked to compile the Holy Quran into a published Book.

Whereas Zaid bin Thabit memorized the whole Quran by heart, he did not submit any Verses to the formed Book unless he had acquired two witnesses for each Verse-- their testimonies were in written form and memorization--to confirm the Verses were exactly like how they were revealed ensuring no words or letters were added or subtracted from the text.

It's important to stress that the Prophet's main scribe, Zayd bin Thabit, did not rely on himself, or for that matter, a single companion, to compile the Holy Quran. Instead, he called upon the services of the many memorizers of the Holy Quran to ensure and confirm that they possessed the exact Verses of the Holy Quran, as sent down and Revealed to Prophet Muhammad PBUH with no additions or subtractions.

Many companions of the Prophet PHUH memorized the Holy Quran during the life of the Prophet, word for word. The companions knew that past Scriptures, such as the Torah sent with Prophet Moses and the Gospel sent with Jesus Christ, were rendered lost, so they took the necessary steps to protect the Holy Quran from any additions, enhancements, or subtractions; doing so through the devices of word for word memorization.

No parts of the Holy Quran were lost when Zaid bin Thabit compiled the Quran into book form; this owing to the fact that the companions had written copies of the Holy Quran, and the Holy Quran as a whole was memorized by many of the companions. The oral tradition has always been the primary means of preserving the Holy Quran; even today, millions of people worldwide have memorized the Quran by heart. This more than 600-page document is memorized word for word, letter for letter, even by children that do not speak Arabic. Even if every single copy of the Quran were to be burnt today, it would not matter--because many people worldwide have the Holy Quran memorized by heart.

This complete Book of the Holy Quran remained with the first Caliph, Abu Bakr, until his death, then was passed down to the second Caliph, Umar ibn Al Khattab. After his death, it was entrusted to his daughter, Hafsa, also a wife of the Prophet PBUH.

During the 3rd Caliph of Islam of Uthman ibn Affan, he realized that many non-Arabs were converting to Islam and that the Holy Quran was being recited and written in various dialects and scripts. In addition, some of the companions would compose the Holy Quran from memory or copy its text from someone else with their own hands. This activity often results in human copyist errors.

Since the Arabic language scripture had yet to develop at this point entirely, one letter or symbol can represent multiple letters, increasing the likelihood of a copyist's error. The companions also would sometimes jot down their notes in the margins of their text copies for their own benefit, whether the notes formed the definitions of a word, the pronunciation of a word, a supplication dua, etc. Many of the companions had not learned how to read or write proficiently. The Arabian Peninsula had a high illiteracy rate then, and many of the notes in their codices contained spelling errors.

Uthman ibn Affan deemed it critical that everyone, including future generations, receives the unaltered Message of God in its exact words, verbatim, sans the enhancement or addition of anyone's notes or the presence of copyist errors. It would confuse and confound future generations to receive personalized copies of the Holy Quran, each bearing notes from a companion. To prevent this from happening, the Caliph at the time, Uthman ibn Affan, requested that all of the personal copies of the Holy Quran that contained the individual notes of the companions--be burned, save the single original Quran compiled by the Prophet's main scribe Zaid bin Thabit and the appointed committee. Finally, only one version remained, including the exact Words of Allah verbatim, as the Holy Quran was intended. Uthman ibn Affan standardized all copies of the Holy Quran.

In the West, the ritual of burning something has a negative connotation that represents a show of disrespect or the concealment of evidence. However, this was not the case when the fragments of the Holy Quran containing the companion's notes were burned. In Islam, Muslims cannot simply discard any text that includes the Words of God into the garbage, as such a gesture would be deemed disrespectful. Instead, they must be burnt or buried. It was necessary to burn those copies to ensure they did not circulate to the rest of humanity. Because this same act was not done with the Gospel, the Bible today contains verses that originated as notes in the margin of pages--written by scribes never meant to make them into verses, as they never contained the words of God nor Jesus Christ.

With the original master copy of the Holy Quran in possession of the Caliph Uthman ibn Affan and all personal copies burnt, master copies were made from the original and distributed to each city's grand Mosque in the Islamic province. Recipients included Mecca, Medina, Basra, Kufa, and Damascus, along with the dispatchment of Quran reciters to teach the people in those cities the correct recitation and pronunciation of the text. In addition, the Book's master copies were present in the city's grand Mosque so that people could make copies. From that time until today, every Quran copy in the world has existed in the same version, letter for letter. It is believed that original documents exist today in Turkey and Uzbekistan.

"Indeed, it is We who sent down the Qur'an, and indeed, We will be its Guardian." (Quran 15:9)

God has promised to preserve the Holy Quran, protecting His Book from anyone who attempts to modify or change its Text or Message. This means God will guard His Book against human-made modifications, distortions, additions, subtractions, or tampering.

**"This is the Book about which there is no doubt,
a guidance for those conscious of Allah" (Quran 2:2)**

Are Women Oppressed in Islam?

The media frequently portrays Islam as a religion that oppresses women. Sadly, women are oppressed in a few Muslim countries around the world, but any form of emotional, physical, or psychological abuse or oppression towards women is prohibited in the faith and strongly goes against the teachings and laws of Islam. The suppression of women occurs in many parts of the world, regardless of the oppressor's religion or culture—or even if the oppressor is an atheist. And no Islamic laws exist sanctioning this oppression. Islam specifically states that women have the right to a decent life without facing aggression or abuse, just as men do. The Holy Quran says God the Almighty created all species in pairs, indicating that men and women were created of the same species. Prophet Muhammad, peace be upon him, stated that *Women are the twin halves of men*. Furthermore, God says in the Holy Quran:

"The men believers and women believers are Auliya' (helpers, supporters, friends, protectors) of one another" (Quran 9:71)

Islam states that men and women were created in a pure state, and both are equal in the eyes of God. The only real criterion that judges the superiority of one person over another takes the form of piety, God-consciousness, and righteousness.

**"...Indeed, the most noble of you in the sight of
Allah is the most righteous of you..." (Quran 49:13)**

Men and women of the Islamic faith are expected to fulfill the same
obligations of faith, worship, prayer, charity, etc.—as stressed in the Holy
Quran. Women do not differ from men in the spiritual sense, as both
men and women are subject to God's reward or punishment.

**"And whoever does righteous deeds, whether male or female,
while being a believer - those will enter Paradise and will not be
wronged, even as much as the speck on a date seed"
(Quran 4:124)**

While men and women are spiritually equal in the eyes of God, the
two genders are not identical. They exhibit many biological,
psychological, and physical differences; therefore, comparing their roles
would not be logical. The rights, responsibilities, and roles of each gender
are balanced yet are not necessarily the same. Each gender claims
different roles in life, and each is suited for their respective role according
to their functions, as designed by nature. Men possess more physical
strength than women, which is why men and women compete in separate
athletic competitions in such rigorous sports as boxing or basketball.

"...And the male is not like the female..." (Quran 3:36)

One should not misinterpret these differences to mean that men are
superior or inferior to women; instead, these roles are attributed to each
gender's natural capacity and the proper functioning of each gender. For
example, women are equipped for childbearing, while men are incapable
of giving birth. On the other hand, a man is suited for military field battles
during times of war, while the appointment of a woman to fight in the
field in place of a man would be a disadvantage for the army. Men and
women complement each other while serving as a means of mutual
fulfillment.

Men and women have preferences and advantages related to their genders. The Holy Quran states that men stand at one degree over women. According to Islamic scholars, this edict references the Verse indicating that men are caretakers of women and should fulfill all of their responsibilities in terms of protecting, supporting, and providing for them. This Verse does not imply that men stand as an authority over women. Women are the beneficiaries of this Verse. A woman's role is to comfort and support her man. He who created both men and women knows the capabilities, weaknesses, and strengths of each gender.

In past societies - the Romans, Greeks, and Babylonians, in particular - women were denigrated, used for sex and pleasure, treated as property, and prostituted. Some civilizations even considered women as evil instruments of the devil and deprived them of various basic rights. Some societies even buried baby girls alive after birth. Islam was the first religion to grant women status in society.

In many later societies, men deprived women of their basic inheritance rights and treated them as transferable property. However, Islam gives women the right to own property and receive their just inheritance from relatives. Islam gives women the right to get an education, marry who they please, retain their family name after marriage, divorce, and work outside the home. They have the right to earn their own independent income, start their own business, and vote. Of note, Islam granted these rights to females when they were not the norm in the world and culture. In Islam, the husband cannot touch his wife's money without her permission and must support her and cover the household expenses. Islam introduced the rights of a mother, wife, daughter, etc., into the annals of human culture.

When the Holy Quan was revealed, its scripture condemned sexist attitudes and discrimination against women. Indeed, the Book raised the status of women, honored them, and demonstrated how they could maintain their God-given honor. Nowhere in the Holy Quran will you find a Verse that degrades women or gives them a secondary status. The

51

Holy Quran has an entire chapter named "The Women." There is no chapter called "The Men." The Holy Quran also contains a chapter named "Mary," who is mentioned throughout the Holy Book. Islam's first follower was a woman (Khadijah, the Prophet's wife). The first martyr in Islam was also a woman.

Prophet Muhammad PBUH stated in a Hadith: *The most complete of the believers in faith is the one with the best character among them. And the best of you are those who are best to your women.* (At-Tirmidhi) Another narration contains a statement from Prophet Muhammad PBUH: *Whoever has three daughters, or three sisters, or two daughters, or two sisters, and he keeps good company with them and fears Allah regarding them, then Paradise is for him.* (At-Tirmidhi)

Treating one's parents well, especially the mother, is highly mandated in Islam and the Holy Quran. The Holy Quran elevates mothers to a high status and commands everyone to treat their mothers with the utmost respect, kindness, tenderness, love, devotion, and care. Our Prophet PBUH stated: *Paradise lies under the feet of your mother.* Additionally, when Prophet Muhammad PBUH was asked by a companion, *Who amongst the people is the worthiest of my companionship? Prophet Muhammad PBUH responded, Your mother. Then the man asked, Then who?, and Prophet Muhammad PBUH replied, Your mother and the companion replied, Then who? Prophet Muhammad PBUH replied, Your mother, at which point the companion replied, then who? And finally, Prophet Muhammad PBUH replied, Then your father.*

A Muslima is honored in Islam and Sharia (Islamic Law). While the media often portrays Muslim women as oppressed, weak, and submissive to their husbands based on how they look and dress, the apparel of Muslim women stands as a symbol of their liberation from societal objectification. Non-Muslim women often dress to attract the attention of the opposite gender, while a Muslim woman's goal is to dress appropriately and modestly and to attract the least attention in a world where the physical form is constantly emphasized and given undue focus.

Islam elevates the one who covers herself, safeguarding her integrity by not allowing herself to be treated as a sexual object. She is not to be valued and judged externally, based solely on her appearance, but rather internally on her righteousness, character, mind, and intellect. A Muslim woman does not desire to adorn her body for men, sexualizing herself to gain attention from men other than her husband. Muslim women look up to and identify with Mary, the mother of Prophet Jesus, peace be upon her, known for her piety, righteousness, character, God-consciousness, and modesty.

In today's modern Arabic vernacular, the word *Hijab* refers to a *headscarf.* Yet, in classical Arabic and the language of the Quran, the Hijab refers to a physical curtain, a screen, a partition, or a barrier that separates one from others when one stands behind it. The one being covered by or found behind the hijab is not only covering her head and body but also the space around her as she stands behind a curtain, screen, partition, or barrier. According to the Holy Quran, this garment was an extra layer of coverage required to be worn only by Prophet Muhammad PBUH's wives.

"...And when you ask his wives for something, ask them from behind a partition. That is purer for your hearts and their hearts..." (Quran 33:53)

The Prophet PBUH's wives not only had to cover their heads and bodies, but they had to place covers or curtains in front of them to conceal their space when speaking to men other than their mahrams (a person who that individual may not marry because of their close blood relationship, such as a brother, uncle, nephew, etc.). The Almighty gave additional rules of etiquette regarding how one should speak to the wives of the Prophet PBUH.

The hijab provided an extra layer of privacy while symbolizing noble women's high status and dignity. To reiterate, the classic meaning of the term hijab in the Holy Quran is not the same as the meaning we reference today. The wearing of the Hijab mentioned in the Holy Quran was not required by anyone other than the Prophet PBUH's wives, as outlined in the Holy Quran. Regarding all other Muslim women, a different verse of the Quran explicitly instructs that women wear headscarves.

"And tell the believing women to reduce some of their vision and guard their private parts and not expose their adornment except that which necessarily appears thereof and to wrap a portion of their headcovers over their chests and not expose their adornment except to their husbands, their fathers, their husbands' fathers, their sons, their husbands' sons, their brothers, their brothers' sons, their sisters' sons, their women, that which their right hands possess, or those male attendants having no physical desire, or children who are not yet aware of the private aspects of women. And let them not stamp their feet to make known what they conceal of their adornment. And turn to Allah in repentance, all of you, O believers, that you might succeed" (Quran 24:31)

The Holy Quran uses the word *Khamar* to refer to a headscarf covering the head. Khamar comes from a root word meaning "to cover something." The word Khamar is similar to the Arabic word Kha'mir, the word for alcohol. The consumption of alcohol impairs one's intellect: one cannot think rationally while under the influence, as liquor creates a barrier between the mind and the power of speech and reasoning. God states in His Book, "Tell the believing women to wear their Khomar (the plural of Khamar) over their bosom as in to throw their shawl over and cover their chest area." So, aside from covering one's chest, the head should be covered as well since the concealment of the head is implied through the use of the word Khomar in this Verse. So, the essentials of the Khamar dictate that the hair is to be covered and that cloth covers the women's chest.

Whereas women in the days of the Prophet PBUH would wear headscarves generally, some would expose their chest area by pushing

54

their headscarves back; as a result, they were commanded by God the Almighty to cover their chests as well.

Besides covering the head, neck, and chest area, God instructs the believing Muslim woman to wear a Jilbab, referencing a loose outer garment that does not define their body shape and that conceals their beauty. The garment is worn by Muslima when leaving her home or in the presence of those aside from her mahram.

"O Prophet, tell your wives and your daughters and the women of the believers to bring down over themselves part of their outer garments. That is more suitable that they will be known and not be abused. And ever is Allah Forgiving and Merciful"
(Quran 33:59)

As these Verses in the Holy Quran are very explicit and direct, no disagreements or disputes have been imposed against this edict by Islamic scholarship in the past unless it questions whether women also should cover their faces and feet. The primary reason a Muslim woman wears the Hijab can be attributed to Muslima's belief that her true purpose in life is to worship God the Almighty according to His instructions, as revealed in God's final Revelation to humanity, the Holy Quran and through the teachings of Prophet Muhammad PBUH, the final Messenger of God. Wearing the headscarf and outer garment is an act of righteousness and obedience to God. A Muslim woman wears the Hijab to seek and gain the pleasure of her Master.

It is the core teaching of Islam that, whatever God instructs one to do, it is always best to follow it, whether one understands its logic or not. A Muslim woman trusts God and does what He instructs her to do, trusting it will be best for her. God knows what's best for her more than she does. God is the Creator of everything and is All-Knowing, All-Wise. Only when she submits to God and obeys His commands does the Muslima reap the benefits of her faith, feeling true tranquility and contentment in life, as she knows God is pleased with her. By focusing on and submitting to the demands of God, she is set free and is no longer a slave to and prisoner of society's pressures and desires.

"Whoever does righteousness, whether male or female, while he is a believer - We will surely cause him to live a good life, and We will surely give them their reward in the Hereafter according to the best of what they used to do" (Quran 16:97)

Islam stresses the relationship between the body and the mind. In covering her body, a Muslim woman shields her heart from spiritual impurities. A Muslim woman wears the Hijab to uphold Islam's code of modesty. This code extends to all aspects of life, including her dress and carriage. A Muslim's dress is an outer manifestation of inner purity, beauty, and humility. Wearing the Hijab embodies moral conduct, character, manners, and speech. A Muslim woman guards her modesty and does not attract unnecessary attention, such as leering admiration, praise, or sexual attraction expressed by those other than her husband.

Whereas admiring attention from others may boost the ego for a short period, a Muslim woman acknowledges that this heed can lead to negative consequences in the long term, such as jealousy from others, envy, competition, affairs, acting as a poor role model for children, and possibly a marital breakup--as we so often see in the West and around the world, where dressing immodestly is common.

A Muslim woman boasts the trait of Ha'yaa (modesty, bashfulness, and a sense of shame). She values her beauty, so she veils herself. The Hijab diverts attention from, conceals, and protects the Muslima. God also instructs women to lower their gazes when members of the opposite gender are present, thus showing Haya's trait (bashfulness).

"And tell the believing women to reduce some of their vision and guard their private parts by being chaste ..." (Quran 24:31)

A Muslima is honored in Islam and Sharia (Islamic Law). Islam elevates the one who covers herself, safeguarding her integrity by not allowing herself to be treated as a sexual object. She is not to be valued and judged externally based solely on her appearance but rather internally on her righteousness, character, mind, and intellect. A Muslima woman does not desire to adorn her body for men, sexualizing herself to gain attention from those other than her husband.

**"...That is more suitable that they will be known and not be abused molested. And ever is Allah Forgiving and Merciful..."
(Quran 33:59)**

According to this Verse, a Muslima should wear an outer garment and dress modestly so she can be recognized as a Muslim woman who is chaste and serious about her modesty. A Muslima sets a standard and sends a message to everyone around her that she is not one to sell herself cheaply. She knows her value; she is a strong woman with courage, inner strength, and fortitude. She is a practicing Muslima that would not harm, oppress, or cheat anyone. The Hijab veil and outer garment help prevent a Muslima from being a victim of molestation, taunting, or teasing. She wears modest garb, not only to protect herself but to protect men and society.

Contrary to popular belief, the Hijab is not worn solely to restrain men's illicit desires. It is not the women's responsibility to regulate a man's behavior. Every man is responsible and accountable for his own conduct. The Holy Quran instructs men to be modest, lower their gaze, guard their modesty, and handle themselves sensibly in every sphere of their lives. God states:

"Tell the believing men to reduce some of their vision and guard their private parts. That is purer for them. Indeed, Allah is Acquainted with what they do" (Quran 24:40)

The Holy Quran instructs men to observe modesty when speaking to women. While many often incorporate the concept of the Hijab with wearing a headscarf, this is only one application. The Hijab is more than a head covering; it symbolizes the overall concept of being modest and humble in other aspects of life.

Similar instruction is given in the Bible: *You have heard that it was said, 'You shall not commit adultery.' But I tell you that anyone who looks at a woman lustfully has already committed adultery with her in his heart.* (Gospel of Mathew 5:27-28)

In the Holy Quran, the Almighty specifically addresses women when He asks them not to show off their adornments and to draw their veils over their bodies due to the physical and biological distinctions between males and females and how the female body can be an object of attraction. This is evident in today's commercialized world, where disgraceful, overtly sexualized media is catered overwhelmingly to men as opposed to women by corporations and industries mindful of how their advertising and sale of products influence purchasing behavior.

Some feminist movements and media outlets portray the Hijab as a depiction of the oppression and slavery of women. Sadly, some Muslim women are oppressed in many parts of the world, even though this treatment goes against the teachings of Islam. While a particular government or group of people may oppress women in general, it is not truthful to say that Islam oppresses women. No Islamic laws oppress women; they have every right to a decent life without facing aggression or abuse.

If women were granted their God-given rights, oppression would not exist. Unfortunately, Islam is not being practiced as it should, even in Muslim lands, where the citizens fail to enact the true principles of the religion. Islam honors women, yet sadly and across the globe, Muslim women fall victim to cultural aberrations that have no place in the faith.

A Muslim woman who covers her hair and places her religion above worldly pursuits is labeled as oppressed. Still, a state of oppression is not defined by a piece of material on one's head but rather by a weakening of the heart and mind. Liberation means freedom but not acting recklessly. Freedom must never come at the expense of oneself or others. When a Muslim woman fulfills the role she was created for, to find God, build a relationship with Him, and follow His guidance, she is liberated, empowered, and honored. She is liberated and freed from the shackles of society, its pressures, unrealistic stereotypes, and images dictated by the media. Muslim women who cover their hair and dress modestly view the act as a right, not a burden.

The concept of the Hijab is not unique to Islam. The three Abrahamic religions share many beliefs, including that a woman should cover her hair publicly with a veil. It was the custom of Jewish women and Catholic nuns to go out in public with their heads covered. And as recently as 40-50 years ago, it was unheard of for a Christian woman to go to church without covering her head or wearing a long skirt.

The concept of female head covering is found and mandated in the Bible. If her head is uncovered, the Bible states, she dishonors herself and should have her hair shaved: *But every woman that prayeth or prophesieth with her head uncovered dishonoureth her head: for that is even all one las if she were shaven. For if the woman be not covered, let her also be shorn: but if it be ma shame for a woman to be shorn or shaven, let her be covered.* (1 Corinthians: 11: 5-6)

Unlike the related passages in the Holy Quran, Paul, in this Verse, presents the veil as a sign of man's authority. In his view, a woman wearing a headscarf shows her subordination to men. This sexist perspective of why women should cover their heads reflects the views of a few Western individuals, who think the Hijab is oppressive and a symbol of inferiority and degradation. They subconsciously react to the Judeo-Christian concept of the veil, which symbolizes a woman's subjection to her husband. This is not the case in Islam.

The concept of the Hijab comes accompanied by obligatory conditions for Muslim women to follow. The requirements are: the entire body, except for the face and hands, should be covered by loose and concealing, not tight and transparent clothing. Their dress should not attract attention or accentuate the body, should not be perfumed, should not resemble clothing worn by men or unbelievers, nor should it be overly elegant or ornate.

God claims exceptions to this rule in the form of women no longer capable of bearing children, who no longer desire marriage or sexual relations, and who cannot excite the passions of men. These ladies need not cover themselves to the same degree as other women. They even can remove their outer garment.

"And women of post-menstrual age who have no desire for marriage - there is no blame upon them for putting aside their outer garments but not displaying adornment. But to modestly refrain from that is better for them. And Allah is Hearing and Knowing" (Quran 24:60)

The Prophet of God PBUH praised modest women who guard their chastity and the beauty bestowed upon them by God. Prophet Muhammad PBUH also cursed those who publicly display and flaunt their beauty, stating they would not smell the fragrance of Paradise. Our Prophet PBUH warned us that towards the end of time, women who are dressed inappropriately, turning away from righteousness, will be inclined to do evil, leading others astray--including their husbands.

To my dear believing sister, let not the whispers of Satan mislead and misguide you. Let not Satan drag you from your Creator, the most-Merciful. You must recognize that you cannot negotiate your faith regarding what you should accept and decry. You need to submit fully and willingly and realize, my dear sister, that you are blessed and honored to be amongst the people of La Ala Ila Allah (There is no deity worthy of worship except Allah). Do not procrastinate in adhering to the guidelines assigned to you, as your death can occur anytime, bringing an end to the test of your faith.

The act of not wearing a Hijab or not dressing modestly is a sin, but justifying your actions is much worse. When you instead are honest with yourself and are willing to admit your transgressions, you gain the chance for repentance, change, and forgiveness—feeling guilt because of sin is the first step of repentance. Like any other act of worship, dressing modestly and wearing a Hijab requires faith, sacrifice, discipline, and patience. Dressing modestly strengthens the relationship between you and your Lord.

To my dear sister struggling through your journey of the Hijab, strengthen your prayer rituals to strengthen your connection with God and His Book. By supplicating to Him, you call upon Him, the Almighty, the Most Merciful, to help you. Pray and strengthen your connection with Allah, as these acts will deter you from sins and unlawful acts, giving you the power you need to resist evil elements. Take the first step now, and never surrender your quest for faith.

When you wear the Hijab for God alone, all the while ignoring the outside noise, people's stares, and comments, you realize that this journey is worth the struggle. Pleasing people is a goal you can never achieve, but pleasing your Creator—by contrast--is the ultimate road to contentment and peace. Our Prophet PBUH narrated: *Whoever seeks Allah's pleasure by incurring the wrath of the people, Allah will suffice and protect him from the people. And whoever seeks the people's pleasure by Allah's wrath, Allah will entrust him to the people* (Al-Tirmidhi). Surround yourself with righteous, practicing sisters, and realize that you are too precious to be displayed for each man to see.

Realize, my dear sister, that you and your believing sisters are the last true representatives of femininity on this Earth.

Did Islam Start After Judaism and Christianity?

Is Prophet Muhammad PBUH the Founder of Islam?

Contrary to popular belief, Islam is not a relatively new religion that came into existence only 1400 years ago, back in the 7th century. Islam, in truth, has existed since the first moment humankind set foot on Earth. The final Prophet of humanity, Prophet Muhammad PBUH, was not the founder of Islam--as many people mistakenly believe. Instead, he was sent as the last and final Prophet of God.

He was delivered by God the Almighty to convey His universal and eternal message to our nation - the final nation. When Prophet Muhamad PBUH appeared, he did not bring a new religion. Instead, he cast light upon a faith that already existed. Prophet Muhammad PBUH renewed the preceding monotheistic religion, that which has been preached and taught by every previous Messenger and Prophet of God.

Prophet Muhammad PBUH was only the last and final Prophet, the very seal of the Prophets. Islam is the continuation, the culmination, and the completion of God's universal and eternal message to humanity, as revealed to all of God's previous Messengers and Prophets.

Like all previous Prophets and Messengers of God, Prophet Muhammad PBUH preached and taught Tawheed—the oneness of God. He taught that God Alone is worthy of worship and veneration and is the Creator of all. No other being is worthy of worship, not the Sun, the Moon, or idol.

People have been practicing Islam since the creation of Prophet Adam PBUH. Throughout history, anyone who practiced monotheism, submitted to God's will, and followed the Prophet sent to them was considered a Muslim. Throughout the ages, God the Almighty sent Prophets and Messengers to guide and teach their nations in the way of Islam. All Prophets preached the same general message to their nations. All of God's Messengers and Prophets were Muslims by definition because the term Muslim translates to mean '*those who submit their will to God the Almighty.*'

"He has ordained for you of religion what He enjoined upon Noah and that which We have revealed to you, [O Muhammad], and what We enjoined upon Abraham and Moses and Jesus - to establish the religion and not be divided therein. Difficult for those who associate others with Allah is that to which you invite them. Allah chooses for Himself whom He wills and guides to Himself whoever turns back to Him" (Quran 42:13)

All three major world religions–Islam, Christianity, and Judaism–portray the Prophet Abraham PBUH as an inspiring example of someone who submitted himself entirely to God and worshipped Him alone. As a result, the Prophet Abraham, PBUH, plays a prominent role in history and religion.

The Holy Quran shares stories of Prophet Abraham's firm and steadfast belief in God. He is one who called and preached the oneness of God and rejected the idea of idolatry. However, he later faced various difficult tests and hardships God placed before him, testing his belief and loyalty.

The Holy Quran states that Prophet Abraham PBUH was neither a Jew nor a Christian. Prophet Abraham PBUH could not have been a Jew as the term *Judaism* originates from the name *Judah,* a name belonging to a man who resided in the land of Judea and was the grandson of Prophet Abraham PBUH. How could Prophet Abraham PBUH be a Jew if he was born before his grandson, for which Judaism was named? The term *'Judaism'* is not found anywhere in the Torah.

Prophet Abraham PBUH could not have been Christian since Christianity follows the teachings of Jesus Christ, and Prophet Abraham PBUH was born before Jesus Christ. The term *'Christianity'* is also not found anywhere in the Bible, nor has any Prophet, including Jesus Christ, ever acknowledged it. The word Christianity was introduced much later and never was spoken in the life of Jesus Christ.

The question arises: What was the religion of Prophet Abraham PBUH and all the previous Messengers and Prophets of God up until Prophet Adam PBUT, if not Judaism or Christianity? It was Islam! Islam, by definition, means *the act of submitting fully to God.* This act determined the way of life that God, the Almighty, prescribed to all the previous Messengers, Prophets, and humanity. Islam means the voluntary "submission" or "surrender" to the Will of God, and in exchange, one would acquire peace and contentment in this life and the hereafter.

The Holy Quran states that Prophet Abraham PBUH was indeed a Muslim. As noted a few times already, by definition, a Muslim is someone who submits wholly to God, and—according to this definition--Prophet Abraham PBUH was indeed a Muslim, one that submitted himself to God.

"People of the Book! Why do you dispute with us about Abraham
even though the Torah and the Gospel were not revealed until
after the time of Abraham? Do you not understand? Behold, you
are one of those who have disputed greatly concerning matters
which you knew; why are you now disputing about matters that
you know nothing about? Allah knows it whereas you do not
know. Abraham was neither a Jew nor a Christian; he was a
Muslim, wholly devoted to God. And he certainly was not
amongst those who associate others with Allah in His divinity.
Surely the people who have the best claim to a relationship with
Abraham are those who followed him in the past, and presently
this Prophet and those who believe in him; Allah is the guardian
of the men of faith" (Quran 3:65:68)

Islam teaches the oneness of God. Islam forbids the association of
partners with Him, whether in belief or worship. Islam teaches that Allah
neither begets nor is born. There is, very simply, nothing like Him. Islam
teaches that one should live a righteous life with God consciousness ever
present in mind and heart, always following God's Laws. The one who
lives by this teaching will live in Paradise eternally in the hereafter; the
one who does not could be thrown into a pit of hellfire. This edict always
has served as the Universal Message of the previous Prophets sent by
God, fulfilling the natural predisposition and inclination of the soul in
every person. The Holy Quran teaches that the signs and proofs of God's
Wisdom, existence, and power, are always evident in the world around
us.

God sent Prophet Muhammad PBUH, 600 years after the coming of
Prophet Jesus, intending him as the world's last and final Prophet who
came to correct and renew some deviations in monotheism during a time
when the world lived in darkness and when God's Message was altered
once again. God the Almighty sent his Final Messenger to guide
humanity to a better place and faith. Since the Holy Quran is the final
Testament of God the Almighty, God has taken it upon Himself to

safeguard and protect his final Book from human-made alterations, or any form of corruption, for the good of humanity.

**"Indeed, it is We who sent down the Qur'an,
and indeed, We will be its Guardian" (Quran 15:9)**

The Laws of the Holy Quran now serve to abrogate all previous laws. Islam spread more rapidly throughout the world than any other religion. Within its first hundred years, Islam came to dominate the Middle East, Northern Africa, parts of Asia, and Europe. Islam remains the largest growing religion in the world, despite all the negative publicity and wrongful actions of the few misguided extremists committed in the name of this faith. Now the faith boasts 1.8 billion followers, which equates to 24% of the global population. Islam is not limited to one ethnicity or group of people.

Muslims originate from various ethnic backgrounds, races, cultures, and national origins. And although the world contains more Christians than Muslims, Islam has the most followers actively practicing their faith and its rituals around the globe. The world boasts a higher percentage of Muslims practicing Islam than Christians practicing Christianity. Islam is projected to surpass Christianity by the year 2070 as the largest religious group in the world.

Did Islam Spread by the Sword?

How Did Islam Spread
Throughout the World so Quickly?

As Islam spread quickly throughout the world in such a short period, many assume that the sword spread Islam by way of holy wars. But was this the case? One must distinguish between the Islamic State Empire and the Islamic Faith to understand this. Let's first address the Islamic State Empire.

When leaders of the Empire believed they could offer a system better suited for civilizations, they sometimes enacted their powers to expand their reach to other nations, thus benefiting the people in those nations. Empires spread their system using military force, a method of choice throughout history—as is the case with the many western countries that conquered nations in an attempt to extend their system of democracy to lands where--they believed--people were oppressed. The Islamic State Empire started as a small group of people who eventually grew in number and struggled their way to the top. To a certain extent, the Islamic State Empire expanded just as many other Empires expanded throughout history.

Like every other Empire, the Islamic Empire wanted its reach to flourish through political conquests. Without political conquest, they would not have become and remained a superpower. If nations exist where their people are oppressed, their leaders may be confronted for their wrongdoing--as no people deserve mistreatment. One of Islam's main goals is to establish justice in the land and to invite others to know and accept the Message of God. People can hear the message of God without being forced into its acceptance. It would be a tragedy if the leaders of some nations prevented their peoples from hearing the Message of God.

Conquest was the law of the land, and Empires followed this edict to survive. Although most of the battles that Islams fought were defensive, fighting for the protection of their people, the Islamic Empire did expand its Empire by conquering other lands. The Islamic Empire expanded its justice domain by confronting other unjust Empires and letting others hear about Islam without forcing anyone to accept the faith.

Unlike many other Empires, Islam's many rules ensure that everyone is treated with justice, boundaries are not crossed, and no injustice is done when they conquer a land. Islam prohibits Muslims from oppressing the people in their conquered lands or enslaving and selling them as other Empires did. The living situation of the conquered people should always be better in the wake of their conquest. Scholars state that offensive warfare should be avoided in this modern period and that striking peace treaties with other nations is the right approach.

Now we will address the manner in which the Islamic faith grew so quickly in such a short period. Were the citizens of the lands conquered by the Islamic State forced to convert to Islam? No. Forced conversion is not allowed in Islam, as stated in the Holy Quran:

"Let there be no compulsion in religion, for the truth stands out clearly from falsehood. So whoever renounces false gods and believes in Allah has certainly grasped the firmest, unfailing hand-hold. And Allah is All-Hearing, All-Knowing" (Quran 2:256)

Of course, the possibility of these nations' peoples converting to Islam was a motivational factor for the Muslims to conquer these lands. Still, religious conversion was not the primary reason behind the conquest. Like all other Empires, they conquered land to attain political and economic power, reflecting the goals of other Empires. Barring the conquest of other lands, many people would continue to worship idols, fire, cows, the cross, and other false gods, placing those people in great danger of encountering hellfire in the afterlife. It's imperative to reiterate that an Islamic Empire can expand a land, but forcing a religious conversion or committing genocide is never to play a role in this expansion, unlike the events of the Hindu and Christian crusades. Christian Empires forced citizens of their conquered lands to attend Christian schools and obliged citizens to convert, leave the land, or be killed.

When Muslims conquered lands, they treated the citizens of those lands like their brothers and sisters, spreading the message of Islam and inviting them to follow the faith. If they did not accept it, they would remain followers of their chosen religion and pay a Jizya tax as citizens-- just like the Muslims paid an annual Zakat, the value of which is generally greater than what the non-Muslims would pay under Jizya.

The Jizya tax was necessary to fund public services, like the military, from which both Muslims and non-Muslims benefitted. Non-Muslims also derived many other benefits from paying Jizya, which is discussed in the next chapter.

The Islamic Empire also has the option to participate in the signing of peace treaties with other nations. The Empire never broke a signed peace treaty, as treachery is a severe crime in Islam.

To become Muslim, one must submit voluntarily to God. When Muslims conquered and ruled India for about 800 years, they never forced the Indian people to become Muslim but instead were given the right to practice the religion of their choice. Most Indians chose to remain Hindu in faith. Today, 80% of Indians are Hindu. When the Islamic State expanded to the land of Egypt, until the eleventh century, non-Muslims were dominant in this area. Muslims were, for all intents and purposes, the minority. Muslims also ruled Spain for about 800 years, and in this land, non-Muslims lived peacefully with Muslims and flourished.

Muslims ruled Arabia for more than 1400 years, except for brief periods when French and British forces ruled; yet millions of Arabs, now Christians and Jews, have ancestors who were Christians and Jews. Christian and Jewish minorities reside today in many Islamic countries, such as Egypt, Yemen, Syria, Lebanon, Jordan, and more. Despite the truth of the Islamic Empire conquering their land, the existence of these people who never converted to Islam proves that the sword did not spread Islam.

Indonesia, the world's largest Muslim nation, was not conquered by the Muslim army. Instead, many Indonesians converted to Islam when Muslim traders visited Indonesia for business. The Indonesians were impressed by the Muslim traders' civilized behavior and how honestly and kindly they dealt with them. These newly born friendships sparked their interest in Islam, and after researching the faith, they realized that this religion could emanate only from God and was not manmade. Therefore many converted. The Muslim army never reached the East Coast of Africa, but you will find many Muslims living in this region.

The Holy Quran and Hadith (saying of Prophet Muhammad, PBUH) administer many laws to preserve and teach regarding the treatment of non-Muslims living under Muslim rule with requisite justice and fairness. It allows Christians and Jews to maintain their court system under their Biblical laws, worship whomever they please, and live a life where they are not restricted – the religion appealed to non-Muslims, thus inspiring them to convert.

It's important to note that Islam's numbers have risen due to people's attraction to the faith and what it teaches, not because of the sword. Therefore, the conversion rate from Christianity to Islam does not undergo sudden spikes; instead, it always rises gradually. The Islamic approach to converting people has always been inviting and welcoming in nature, demonstrating Islam through actions and words—not force or violence.

Does Islam Allow Men to Beat their Wives?

n regards to gender relationships, a single Verse is perhaps the most widely misunderstood in the Holy Quran regarding men and women. The Verse States:

"Men are in charge of women by right of what Allah has given one over the other and what they spend for maintenance from their wealth. So righteous women are devoutly obedient, guarding in the husband's absence what Allah would have them guard. But those wives from whom you fear arrogance - first advise them; then if they persist, forsake them in bed; and finally, hit them lightly. But if they obey you once more, seek no means against them. Indeed, Allah is ever Exalted and Grand" (Quran 4:34)

Before one comes to a hasty conclusion, it's imperative to understand that the Holy Quran came down to Prophet Muhammad PBUH and that he then interpreted it for us. It would be problematic and inaccurate for people to interpret Verses individually in isolation without reviewing other Verses of the Quran and Hadith (sayings of Prophet Muhammad, PBUH). One needs to hear the explanation of the Verse from the Prophet Muhammad PBUH.

It also would be problematic to ignore the life story of Prophet Muhammad PBUH, as he lived his life based on the Holy Quran and

Sunnah. The exemplary manner in which he lived his life and dealt with others is a prime example for us to learn from and emulate, as God created him as our best role model.

The Holy Quran provides teachings and guidance regarding all aspects of life. According to Islamic scholars, this Verse offers guidance in extreme and not typical cases. It pertains to a wife rebelling against her husband through immoral acts of lewdness, adultery, or disloyalty to her marriage; for example, through having an affair with another man or committing an act of vulgarity, bringing shame to her family. The Holy Quran advises the husband to advise his wife, reminding her to be conscious and fear God. This process of inquiry also may include a course of professional counseling.

If time passes and the issue does not improve through advice and counseling, the husband can continue to sleep in their bed but should abstain from having intercourse with his wife. After some time, if her behavior still does not improve, then as a last resort, the husband would display his concern by tapping her lightly with a small twig the size of a pen, inflicting no pain but making a meaningful symbolic gesture. This gesture symbolizes his disgruntled state, showing her his upset and anger by awakening her and warning her of the gravity of the situation in which she now finds herself. We learn this from our Prophet Muhammad PBUH.

It's imperative to emphasize that this light tapping is a last resort, a remedy intended to fix the situation before the problem leads to divorce, breaking up the family. It's also important to emphasize that this light tapping is only symbolic and is intended to show her the grave severity of the situation. This light tapping must leave no marks or swelling in its wake. The faith of Islam does not allow a man to abuse or strike his wife - or any woman - and many Islamic teachings decree the seriousness of this matter.

One must realize that it would not be uncommon or at all shocking for men, who sometimes are prone to violence, to lose their cool and hit their wives if they catch them in the act of infidelity. This Verse guides husbands, telling them that they may not harm their wives; instead, they should express their disapproval and anger in a way that their wives understand their pain. The Arabic verb in this Verse, "Tharb," is incorrectly translated in English to mean hit or beat or strike-- but these words hold a different, much more harsh connotation than what the Verse is referring to.

Husbands never must abuse this Verse, as it applies to rare, extreme cases in which the wife is out of control. At the time of the Prophet Muhammad, PBUH, some of his companions misinterpreted and misapplied it. A group of women approached the wives of Prophet Muhammad, PBUH, complaining that their husbands beat them. Once Prophet Muhammad, PBUH, heard, he replied: *"Those men are not the best of you,"* Numerous narrations of Prophet Muhammad, PBUH, prohibit any beating or aggressive force against women. Prophet Muhammad, PBUH, stated, *"Do not beat the female slaves of Allah"* (Sunan Ibn Majah 1985).

Prophet Muhammad PBUH is a role model for all husbands, and humanity is to learn from him and emulate how he conducted himself and lived his life. Prophet Muhammad PBUH's wife, Aisha, said he struck none of his wives or servants. Prophet Muhammad, PBUH, instructed that kind treatment was the only way to honor one's wife. He said: *"The best of you is the one who is best to his wife, and I am the best of you to my wives"* (Sunan Ibn Majah 1977).

No act of domestic violence committed by a Muslim to his wife could be traced back to any text from the Holy Quran or the sayings of Prophet Muhammad, PBUH because no such verses exist. If a Muslim is found abusing his wife, he is not adhering to the rulings of Islam, which are given to him by His Creator, the All-High, and Prophet Muhammad, PBUH. If you look at Muslim judges who based their decisions and sentences based on the Holy Quran and Sunnah throughout history, you will find that when a man strikes his wife, he is punished; because no such acts are allowed in our beautiful religion of Islam.

The Bible, by contrast, allows a master to beat his male or female servant half to death with no punishment because the servant is considered their property. *"Anyone who beats their male or female slave with a rod must be punished if the slave dies as a direct result, but they are not to be punished if the slave recovers after a day or two since the slave is their property" Exodus 21:20-21.*

Do Islamic Inheritance Laws Favor Men Over Women?

Why Do Women Receive Half the Inheritance Share of a Man?

"Allah commands you regarding your children: the share of the male will be twice that of the female. If you leave only two or more females, their share is two-thirds of the estate. But if there is only one female, her share will be one-half. Each parent is entitled to one-sixth if you leave offspring. But if you are childless and your parents are the only heirs, then your mother will receive one-third. But if you leave siblings, then your mother will receive one-sixth—after the fulfilment of bequests and debts. Be fair to your parents and children, as you do not fully know who is more beneficial to you. This is an obligation from Allah. Surely Allah is All-Knowing, All-Wise" (Quran 4:11)

I slam is more than a religion; it is a way of life that guides humanity in all aspects of their lives, including providing guidance on inheritance. Islamic law allows a person to leave one-third of their assets to whomever they wish, as long as the beneficiaries are not amongst the remaining two third. The will is implied after the deceased's funeral expenses and outstanding debts are paid.

The remainder two-thirds goes to the beneficiaries listed in Chapter 4 of the Holy Quran—a passage that some non-Muslims find controversial. Whereas Chapter 4 states that the share of a male is twice that of a female, females do not always receive less than males in all circumstances. There are certain instances where both male and female beneficiaries receive the same amount, where women receive more than male and scenarios where females get a share and men get nothing.

In many religions, women do not inherit from their families in any circumstance. At many points throughout history, women did not inherit anything from their families. They were considered property, part of the inheritance estate needing to be married off and relocated. On the other hand, Islam gave women their inheritance rights, stating that their reasonability determines their share--and not their gender.

In some circumstances, females inherit half of what males inherit—but not on all occasions. There is logic and fairness to reinforce those instances in which males get a higher inheritance share than females—with these conditions given to us by our Creator, the All-Knowing, All-Wise, the All-Just.

Because Islam has assigned males as the heads of the household, those who bear the family's financial burden, the men will often spend much of what they inherit back into the family. On the other hand, females are entitled to the entirety of their inheritance and wealth--and their husband's wealth. Women can keep 100% of their inheritance without spending or sharing it with anyone--even if they are wealthy and their husband is poverty-stricken.

God has chosen men to be the guardian of their wives and family, whom they must look after and to whom they must provide food, clothing, shelter, etc. The man must care for and provide for those closest to him. For instance, a husband needs to look after his wife and offspring; if he passes away or neglects his duty, the next man in a woman's life will need to step up and care for the family, whether it's the adult son or the brother of the woman. It's important to stress once again that the reasonability of the sexes determines the share of an inheritance, not the gender.

As a clarifying example, suppose the parents of a son and daughter die, leaving fifteen thousand dollars behind. The daughter would inherit five thousand dollars by edict of Muslim law, and the son would inherit ten thousand dollars. However, if she is unmarried, the brother would have to share the $10,000 with his family, including his wife, children, and even his sister.

In contrast, the daughter can retain the entire $5,000 and is under no obligation to spend any of it on anybody else. The male also has the economic responsibility of paying the mahr or dowry. As stated before, whereas a son gets a larger inheritance percentage than a daughter in this circumstance, this would not apply in other cases; for example, where women do not have the benefit of male breadwinners or may have more dependents. It would depend upon the family's unique financial circumstances and other factors at play. A male would receive more than a female when a male is more closely related to the deceased than a female. For instance, a son of the deceased would get more than a niece. The rules regarding Islamic inheritance are complex and involve a complicated science to comprehend and enact.

These guidelines are put in place to ensure that the inheritance recipients are treated with justice and fairness and that women do not get mistreated--as they would often be in the past and by the law of other religions. Islamic Law recognizes and fully protects women's rights in all stages of life, including before marriage, after marriage, and in the event of a divorce, ensuring their financial security. Women are entitled to receive marital gifts, keep their income as they see fit, own properties, own a business, engage in business transactions, be educated, be entitled to child support, vote, and engage in political and legal affairs. In addition, a married woman keeps her maiden name instead of inheriting her husband's family name. If Muslim women are not allowed their God-given rights in certain Muslim countries, that is not because Islam forbids it; instead, it means that the country is not fully implementing the Creator's laws.

Is a Women's Testimony
Worth Half of That of a Man in Islam?

There is a misconception that a woman's testimony is worth half of that of a man in Islam. This can be traced to Verse 2:282 in the Holy Quran, which states that two men are to be called upon to witness a financial contract; if two men are not available, then one man and two women would suffice. So, two women would testify in place of a single male witness:

"O believers! When you contract a loan for a fixed period of time, commit it to writing... Call upon two of your men to witness. If two men cannot be found, then one man and two women of your choice will witness—so if one of the women forgets the other may remind her...." (Quran 2:282)

When reading this Verse, one can conclude that a woman's testimony is worth only half of that of a man and that women are more prone to forgetting or making errors. However, the requirement of two women to replace one man exclusively refers to the witness of financial agreements and is not meant to be a general stipulation. The ruling of substituting two women for one man is not a statement that men are superior to women but has to do with social and cultural situations at the time the

Holy Quran was sent down to humanity. At the time, women were not educated to be as literate as men. They were not involved in business transactions regarding trading caravans, making them prone to forget contractual details or making administrative errors. They were not as familiar with debt contracts and did not engage in their creation as often as men.

It's human nature to have a weak memory of a matter you are less familiar with and in which you are not frequently involved. Men once handled all business trades while women stayed home, raising children. Asking two women to testify regarding financial contracts in place of one man was vital to protecting the money involved in the financial agreement. The Holy Quran takes the protection of financial contractors seriously.

In certain circumstances, a woman might have witnessed a debt contract, but may not be able to testify in court in front of a judge due to a condition of pregnancy, nursing, childbirth, etc., so a second female witness was sent to back up her witness. The second female witness can also be there for moral support, her presence lessening the likelihood of the first witness being intimidated, strengthening and protecting the female witness.

In short, the requirement of two women to substitute for one man is not a universal rule; it applies only to financial contracts. The Holy Quran speaks about witness testimony in numerous passages, with no specification of the gender of the witness made, except for the single Verse explicitly referring to financial transactions. In other scenarios, female testimony is equal to a man's; in some cases, a woman's testimony is weighted more than a man's. And sometimes, in the case of issues specific to women, only a woman's testimony is allowed.

Regarding this matter, one must understand the difference between witnessing a contract and testifying before a judge. A witness is present during the writing of a contract. Someone giving testimony goes before a judge in the case of a dispute between the two parties involved in an agreement. The Verse in question in this chapter is about women witnessing a contract and not testifying before a judge. A woman's testimony before a judge is equal to the worth of a man's. This Verse only references witnessing a contract, not someone's testimony before a judge.

By no means is this Quranic ruling devaluing the reliability of a woman's testimony, nor does it state that a woman's intellect is less than that of a man. In Islam, a woman's testimony is equal to a man's. The highest and most important form of testimony is related to religion and is far more critical than a testimony regarding a financial contract. If one witness a saying of Prophet Muhammad, PBUH, known as hadith, and passes it down, no distinction is made between men and women witnesses: their testimonies are equal. The Prophet PBUH's Wife, Aisha, is among the top narrators of hadith, and no one ever stated that her reports were worth half of that of a man. Her narrations were valued more than that of her other companions. Indeed, Prophet Muhammad PBUH and his companions took the sole testimony of women in many matters.

Why Can Muslim Men Marry Up to Four Wives?

"If you fear you might fail to give orphan women their due rights
if you were to marry them, then marry other women of your
choice—two, three, or four. But if you are afraid you will fail to
maintain justice, then content yourselves with one or those
bondwomen in your possession. This way you are less likely to
commit injustice" (Quran 4:3)

Polygamy is a marriage system that allows one person to marry
more than one spouse. This system of the marital union comes
in two varieties. In a union of polyandry, a woman marries more
than one man, which is not permissible in Islam - and for good reason.
The other type is polygyny, a system where a man marries more than one
woman, a union acceptable in Islam with certain restrictions.

When the Holy Quran came down, polygyny was practiced in Arabia.
Islam did not introduce the concept of polygyny; instead, the faith
sanctioned regulations and restrictions in a society with no limit imposed
on the number of women a man could marry simultaneously. These
restrictions were intended to protect women and restore justice. Islam
did not mandate polygyny, nor did the faith encourage it.

At a time in Arabia when men guardians would marry numerous
orphans in their custody without regard or offer them their fair dower.

And after battles in which multiple male casualties occurred, leaving widows and female orphans without guardians, the Holy Quran revealed guidance regarding the fair treatment of female orphans to ensure they get fair treatment, their fair share of a dower, and not get taken advantage of.

Marriage in Islam is a transfer of responsibility from the father to the husband, ensuring the husband will provide for the woman involved. In special cases, the Holy Quran allows a man to marry a female orphan, affording a higher likelihood that the man will accept his financial responsibility toward her.

The Holy Quran states if one can treat each wife fairly and equally, he can marry up to four wives. Whereas Allah allows polygyny, He says in the same chapter that it will never be possible for a husband to treat all his wives with equitable fairness. He warns men to exercise caution before entering a polygeny relationship, as it is no easy task to treat multiple wives fairly and do them all justice. In such a relationship, men can encounter problems with their wives and Allah. This issue limits the possibility of polygyny in societies. Thus, Allah indirectly implies that monogamy is preferred in most cases.

"You will never be able to maintain emotional justice between your wives—no matter how keen you are. So do not totally incline towards one leaving the other in suspense. And if you do what is right and are mindful of Allah, surely Allah is All-Forgiving, Most Merciful." (Quran 4:129)

Polygyny is not a required marital state; it's optional. A tiny percentage of Muslims practice polygyny. Some Muslim countries prohibit polygyny, some restrict it, and some allow it. Whereas the practice has its negative aspects, its positives and benefits outweigh the negatives, and the union resolves issues facing certain societies. Polygyny may not be suitable for everyone at their current place and time, but it sometimes makes sense to marry more than one wife.

While monogamy is generally the preferred norm for contemporary marriages, certain societies in the past boasted more female residents than men because of the high mortality rate of men dying in war or from violent crimes. Some communities have seen female residents outliving their spouses due to the latter being exposed to dangerous occupations or activities that put their health at risk or because women generally boast stronger immune systems than men.

The increased rate of homosexual activity in men could increase the likelihood of women not getting married in their communities. Considering these issues, polygyny can be a solution to prevent the abandonment of women who have no men to support them financially and take care of their needs. If one man married only one woman in those communities, it would deny women the chance to get married and live a normal life.

Whereas one might think that the state of monogamy protects women's rights, some societies in which polygyny is prohibited deny support to their female citizens, forcing them to resort to prostitution and unlawful relationships while also leaving a populace of children to be raised only by their mothers. Societies that ban polygyny are often plagued with many extramarital affairs among citizens. Polygyny also can be an alternative to divorce when a man is married to a sick or infertile wife and wants to bear a child.

Polygyny is not exclusive to Islam; the Old Testament, New Testament, and Hindu Scriptures all decree that men can marry an unlimited number of wives. The New Testament does not prohibit polygyny, save for Bishops and Deacons. According to the Bible, Prophet Abraham PBUH had three wives, Prophet Suliman PBUH had 700 wives and 300 concubines, and Prophet Moses, Jacob, and David PBUT had multiple spouses.

According to Hindu Scriptures, King Dasharatha, the father of Rama and Krishna, had numerous wives. Buddhists also practice polygamy. It wasn't until more recent years that the Church restricted the marriage of more than one wife for a man. And it wasn't until later that a Jewish Rabbi, not God, issued an edict against marriage to more than one wife for a man. The Holy Quran is the only scripture that states a man should marry only one woman if they fear they might not treat each wife fairly and justly.

What is Sharia Law in Islam?

Do Muslims Want to Spread Islamic Sharia Law to Non-Muslim Countries?

Among the most misunderstood and abused terms and concepts of Islam, both by non-Muslims and Muslims alike is the Sharia Law. Sharia is often portrayed in the media as evil and barbaric, an evil that extremists and terrorists follow, preach, and try to spread in the West. The media often do this for political reasons.

The term "Sharia" linguistically originates from an Arabic word meaning "a path that leads to a watering place." Figuratively, the word refers to a clear, straight path. In Islam, Sharia Law means Divine legislation, the infallible law of God, as opposed to human legislation. Sharia is a set of Divine laws and ethics that Muslims live by to draw closer to God and to live in justice and kindness in honor of His Creation.

"And We have revealed to you, [O Muhammad], the Book in truth, confirming that which preceded it of the Scripture and as a criterion over it. So judge between them by what Allah has revealed and do not follow their inclinations away from what has come to you of the truth. To each of you We prescribed a law and a method. Had Allah willed, He would have made you one nation [united in religion], but He intended to test you in what He has given you; so race to all that is good. To Allah is your return all together, and He will then inform you concerning that over which you used to differ" (Quran 5:48)

No society can function without rules and regulations; without legal boundaries, society will dissolve into anarchy and chaos. Most religions feature sacred Divine laws and ethics equivalent to Islam's Sharia - for instance, Judaism's Halakah Law and the Catholic's Canon Law. Shariah provides the legal framework for the healthy foundation and functioning of society. The religion of Islam incorporates a set of rules and regulations that protects and preserves the rights and freedoms of individuals and society. It is a doctrine concerned with justice, equality, and respect for all.

The Sharia Law is derived from the Holy Quran, its primary source, and the Sunnah (teachings of Prophet Muhammad PBUH), a secondary source. Laws of Sharia also come from Islamic Scholars, who, in their conveyance of the law, draw upon an interpretative process that includes Qiyas (reasoning by analogy, derived from the primary sources), Ijma (the consensus of the opinions held by the Prophet's companions and agreements reached by Islamic scholars), and Ijtihad, the effort to arrive at one's own judgment or reasoning to seek the answers that go unaddressed by the Holy Qur'an and Sunnah. Of these five sources, the first two are Divine, while the other three (Qiyas, Ijma, and Ijtihad) are humanistic efforts based on independent juristic reasoning.

Sharia Law is applied to protect and preserve five basic rights: the right to practice religion, the protection of Muslim and non-Muslim life, the safeguarding of the mind/intellect/reason, the preservation of honor, dignity, and family, and the sanctity of wealth and property. The Sharia aims to secure humanity's welfare and establish a righteous society.

Shariah is more than just Islamic Law; it is not limited to legal issues. Sharia deals with ethical, moral, political, and social codes of conduct for Muslims at the individual and communal levels. Sharia deals with every aspect of life, such as economics, politics, crime, diet, spirituality, hygiene, sexual intercourse, and more. These laws tell Muslims precisely what God expects from them and how they can please Him.

Man was created solely to worship and serve God, and without the guidance of God showing the right path, no one can achieve this purpose. These laws tell Muslims precisely what is permissible to do, eat, and drink and how to dress, sleep, and even relieve themselves. These laws also outline what Muslims are not permitted to do.

Sharia law addresses personal religious observances such as prayer, charity, fasting, and God-consciousness. The Sharia also addresses issues such as paying alms to the poor and needy, being good to one's parents, business affairs, inheritance, and marriage. These laws and their inherent ethics encourage Muslims to be God-conscious, kind, respectful, merciful, generous, and compassionate. A Muslim submits, acknowledges, and understands that Allah the Glorious knows what's best for them in all areas of life, so he follows His Laws.

Since the Sharia is concerned with protecting and preserving the rights and freedoms of individuals and communities, the law must contain rules, regulations, and punishments to address and redress misdeeds. Islam imposes laws and penalties on those that transgress. To preserve the goodness of life, Islam prescribes the law of retribution; to safeguard the mind, Islam prescribes punishment to deter drinking and using intoxicants; to preserve family lineage, the faith prescribes the punishment of fornication; and to protect wealth and property, Islam prescribes the punishment for theft.

Like many countries, Sharia Law also allows for the penalty of criminal laws as a form of a deterrent from illegal acts. At the state level, Sharia Law can impose specific punishments for major crimes like killing, adultery, or theft, such as cutting off a hand. Whereas Sharia addresses national laws, these regulations form only a tiny portion of the Sharia. They can be applied only by an Islamic State or Caliphate, which Muslims have maintained in their homelands for centuries.

These laws were purely discretionary, and it is essential to note that not a single incident involving the stoning of an adulterer occurred during the first 1,000 years of Prophet Muhammad PBUH's life. The administration of these laws involved a whole and fair process of prosecution.

One may find some Islamic Laws to be harsh: for example, the punishment for treason, when one deceptively betrays his country's trust, is death; but if Islam didn't level strict laws for treachery, society would be in harm's way constantly. Hence, strict laws are necessary to protect the community and deter dangerous crimes. When you study Islam and Sharia Law, you'll notice that its rulings are based on mercy and compassion. Crimes committed by people do not harm or affect God, but the victims of these crimes suffer. Their rights are violated and need to be restored.

Anyone accused of a crime must be tried and convicted in the Islamic State of Law before punishment is administered. And only a Muslim judge can carry out the sentences for these violations. It is not permissible for individual Muslims to carry out the penalties for these sentences, as there is no place for vigilantism in Islam, which can lead to chaos and injustice.

Western Muslims do not believe that Sharia Law should be applied in the West, in non-Muslim countries. Muslims do not have the secret intention of overtaking Western countries to apply Sharia Law by force. Muslims living in the West and other non-Muslim countries must obey the law of the land, providing that those laws do not bar them from practicing their religion.

Muslims can be true both to their faith and their home country. Muslims cannot enforce or impose Sharia or Islam on anyone who does not wish to follow their mandates; such a dictatorial act would not be permissible in Islam. Nor do western Muslim organizations seek to establish a global caliphate or Islamic State. Muslims seek merely to follow Sharia in their personal and spiritual lives. A Muslim's job is to live the best way possible and be a good role model and representative of Islam for non-Muslims. A Muslim's life task is to relay the Message of Islam with his actions and words without force.

"There shall be no compulsion in acceptance of the religion..."
(Quran 2:256)

Penal Codes in Islam; What's the Deal with Hand Cutting, Lashing, & Stoning?

"...These are the limits set by Allah, so do not approach them..."
(Quran 2:187)

Sharia Law is Divine Legislation consisting of individual laws that deal with the civil aspects of life, including character, dealing with others, prayer, purification, repentance, marriage, divorce, business dealings, etc. Sharia Law also consists of state-based laws regarding the running of a State. Since Sharia protects and preserves the rights and freedom of individuals and societies, its law must contain rules, regulations, and punishments for those that transgress and infringe on people's rights and freedoms.

Listed within state-based laws is a small component known as Hudud-- criminal law and indicates the penal code of Islam. Hudud can be translated as punishment for encroaching upon the limits and boundaries set by Allah. Since certain aspects of Hudud violate human rights, punishments must be enacted to serve justice for those harmed, as is the case in all countries today. Since these crimes severely impact society, they come complete with severe punishments. It's essential to enact harsh penalties for severe crimes, to help deter and discourage such crimes for the community's security.

It's imperative to note that ordinary Muslims cannot enforce the laws we will discuss; these punishments can be carried out only by a Muslim ruler or judge. A person accused of a crime must be tried in an Islamic court and proven guilty before any punishment is implemented. There is no place for vigilantism in the faith of Islam, acts in which Muslims take the law into their own hands.

Instead of throwing someone in a jail cell in a harsh environment alongside other criminals to allow them to network with each other while costing citizen taxpayers a great deal of money, Islam prevents crimes in a different matter by using the Hudud punishments as a form of deterrence and retribution.

It's imperative to note that the chief principle in implementing Hudud punishments is maximizing mercy - seeking to reform the criminal and allowing the doors of repentance to be opened. Hudud punishments are challenging to prove and enforce. A rigorous requirement of solid evidence almost renders these punishments a scare tactic.

A Muslim ruler or jurist can consider many ambiguities to avoid applying a hudud punishment. Prophet Muhammad PBUH stated: *Avert the legal penalties from the Muslims as much as possible if he has a way out, then leave him to his way, for if the Imam makes a mistake in forgiving it would be better than making mistake in punishment'* As Hudud laws are very difficult to execute, not a single incident of stoning an adulterer occurred in the first 1000 years of the life of Prophet Muhammad PBUH. And only three or four incidents are recorded of lashings in this faith.

"As for male and female thieves, cut off their hands for what they have done— a deterrent from Allah. And Allah is Almighty, All-Wise" (Quran 5:38)

Islam takes the rights of people's property very seriously, and as a result, the religion enacts laws to protect any act of aggression toward other people's property. The Islamic concept of theft is to "take that which does not belong to you stealthily from a place where similar things are typically kept." Without a severe punishment for theft, this evil would spread throughout society. Harsh punishment is needed as a deterrent to scare people away from such an evil act.

The punishment for theft is to cut off the perpetrator's hands at the wrist joint, where the hand meets the forearm. Cutting the hands of thieves was a practice in Arabia before the inception of Islam, and the Holy Quran ratified the practice. It's imperative to note that we don't randomly cut off the hands of all thieves. More than sixty conditions must be met to warrant an amputation verdict. The thief must be given a fair trial and presumed innocent until proven guilty.

Two witnesses of upright character must attest and agree with one another's testimony. The thief must be released if there are no witnesses to the alleged crime. If the thief admits to stealing and is forgiven by the property owner, his hands are not chopped off. The value of the stolen good must exceed a specific value, worth a quarter of a Dinar or more, so the chopping off of hands doesn't apply as a punishment for petty theft. The thief must be a sane adult who committed the crime of his own free will, not under duress, drunk, or motivated by hunger. The stolen property would have had to have been stored in a secure place like a drawer, safe, or cupboard. Other conditions need to be met as well.

If the thief can prove he stole out of need, the Muslim government would not only stop the punishment but also be required to help the thief meet his living needs. It is nearly impossible for a thief to be sentenced unless he confesses twice and doesn't retract his statement, which is why the chopping-off hands have rarely occurred in history. Due to the severity of this harsh punishment, the theft rate was very low in places where this penalty was enforced. The chopping off of the hands is also referenced in the Bible in Deuteronomy 25: 11-12.

"As for female and male fornicators, give each of them one hundred lashes, and do not let pity for them make you lenient in enforcing the law of Allah if you truly believe in Allah and the Last Day. And let a number of believers witness their punishment" (Quran 24:2)

The act of intercourse between a man and woman with no legitimate marital relationship is prohibited in Islam. It is considered a grave sin because the act severely affects individuals and society. The preservation of lineage is important, and the commission of intercourse outside marriage can cause a child to be born who will never know their father's identity. Someone who grows up without a father can lose their God-given inheritance rights and other rights. The intercourse outside of marriage does not ensure that a woman and her newborn will be taken care of financially by the baby's father. An increase in incidents of intercourse outside of marriage can cause unplanned pregnancies and sexually transmitted diseases.

"And do not come near to adultery; surely it has been an obscenity and odious as a way" (Quran 17:32)

The Holy Quran states that the person who engages in fornication is to be lashed 100 times for their crime. Scholars say that this Verse refers to unmarried people. Married people who cheat on their spouses are to be stoned, as stated in Hadith. For these punishments to be implemented, four witnesses of the physical act must come forward who have no doubts as to what they witnessed. For the act to bear four witnesses, it would have to have been committed in public. Many countries have laws regarding this variety of crimes, known as a public display of indecency. This is a serious crime, as children and innocent people can witness it; it can potentially traumatize or corrupt them. Some scholars state that this Verse refers to those who repeatedly perform an act of intercourse outside of marriage, like prostitutes or those who work in the pornography industry. Of course, these industries are very harmful to society.

For any testimony to be accepted, it must be delivered by four sane Muslim adult witnesses with integrity who saw the physical act of the adulterer's penis as it penetrated the woman's vagina, leaving no room for doubt. In addition, other conditions must be met for someone to be lashed 100 times.

Those who implement the punishment of 100 lashes have rules to abide by to ensure they are not committing any injustice to the offender. The one performing the lashing should not raise their arm high enough to reveal their armpits, as that would cause more pain. They should not whip anyone on an exceptionally hot or cold day, as that could cause more pain. The lashing is not meant to cause permanent damage or to kill. That is not what Allah intends for the one being punished.

"Those who accuse chaste women of adultery and fail to produce four witnesses, give them eighty lashes each. And do not ever accept any testimony from them—for they are indeed the rebellious" (Quran 24:4)

Making a false accusation against an innocent person regarding adultery or other immoral act is a severe sin due to the harm it can cause the person and society. Anyone who accuses a Muslim of adultery without providing four witnesses to the act will get a punishment of eighty lashes to protect the community from this crime, safeguard people's honor, and more. And the one who submitted the false accusation would be disqualified as a witness in other cases.

Jihad, Holy War and Terrorism in Islam

slam is a greatly misunderstood faith, especially in the western world, and no Islamic term is more widely misunderstood and decried as the word Jihad. Jihad often is mistranslated to mean Holy War. Some non-Muslims misunderstand the term to indicate the waging of war against disbelievers, to convert them to Islam or kill them. Often, the word Jihad is thought to be synonymous with terrorism, but this couldn't be further from the truth.

Jihad comes from an Arabic word meaning "to make an effort" or "to strive towards a goal." Jihad means " exerting oneself" or "to struggle." In the Islamic context, it means to struggle against one's evil inclination. So, any effort of self-improvement, whether enhancing one's spirituality, education, or financial situation, is an act of Jihad.

"We shall certainly guide those who strive for Our cause to Our path. God is certainly with the righteous ones" (Quran 29:69)

This Verse applies to one who spiritually struggles to attain closeness to and seek the pleasure of God. Jihad comes in different forms. The essential Jihad, known as Major Jihad, is Jihad An-Nafs (the Jihad of the soul). This is the spiritual struggle between two powers within humans: the soul and the body. The soul is prone to becoming corrupt from within oneself, external influences, or both sources.

"Verily, the soul is inclined to evil" (Quran 12:53)

Islam expresses the importance of purifying, cleansing, and restraining oneself from submitting to sinful desires. Islam expects its followers to prefer their souls and conscience instead of their bodies and desires by striving to resist urges and inner temptations. They are expected to avoid acts of disobedience and instead perform acts of obedience pleasing to God.

"And whoever strives only strives for the benefit of himself. Indeed, Allah is free from need of the worlds" (Quran 29:6)

Islam emphasizes self-improvement, self-development, self-restraint, and self-control to shape one's life in the best manner for personal benefit and the good of society. This Jihad is intended to purify the soul. The concept involves struggling against the greed for worldly purposes, arrogance, pride, envy, jealousy, hatred, hypocrisy, insincerity, vanity, narcissism, and other evil traits Satan uses to lead humanity astray into destruction. Every Muslim must strive daily to overcome these evils to the best of their ability. The Jihad of the soul includes the struggle to perform good deeds to please God and become closer to Him. Allah states in His Book:

"He has succeeded who purifies it." (Quran 91:9)

Scholars state that the successors to whom this Verse refers are those individuals who purify their souls by obeying God and restraining from sins and evil doing. The other primary Jihad is Jihad Al-Shaytan (Jihad against Satan). Satan's main aim is to destroy the religion of humanity by attacking them with continuous whispers regarding their belief in God and to tempt, corrupt, and mislead people away from God's guidance.

"O, you who have believed, enter into submission completely and perfectly and do not follow the footsteps of Satan. Indeed, he is to you a clear enemy" (Quran 2:208)

The whispers of Satan come to both righteous people and the wicked. These whispers can be detrimental to one's spiritual, emotional, physical, and psychological well-being. One needs to fight against Satan, warding off the doubts the demon stirs up that undermine faith in God and resisting the corrupt desires he provokes.

These two types of Jihad are the foundation of all other varieties of the concept of Jihad and are obligatory for everyone to be held accountable. If one does not engage in these types of Jihad, one cannot venture into the other realm of Jihad, which involves battles against external enemies.

This introduces us to the other type of Jihad, which can be classified as Minor Jihad: the armed struggle against those who plot against Muslims. When Muslims, their faith, or their territory are threatened or attacked, they can defend themselves. This Jihad empowers one to strive on the battlefield and fight in self-defense to protect one's life, family, faith, wealth, and property. The concept addresses the fight against evil, operation, and tyranny to defend what is right and combat oppression. This Jihad equals the effort and struggles to improve society.

Jihad does not equate to Holy War. The Arabic word for Holy War is *Harbun Muqaddasah*. Jihad does not imply Holy War, and the words Holy War do not exist in the Holy Quran or any authentic Hadith (the sayings of Prophet Muhammad PBUH). Killing innocent people—Muslim or non-Muslim—is condemned in Islam and considered a major sin. Islam does not permit Muslims to fight against non-Muslims solely based on their faith. Islam is a religion of peace, mercy, and forgiveness. No one can be compelled to accept Islam.

"There shall be no compulsion in acceptance of the religion. The right course has become clear from the wrong. So, whoever disbelieves infalse deities and believes in Allah has grasped the most trustworthy handhold with no break in it. And Allah is Hearing and Knowing" (Quran 2:256)

Muslims must convey and establish evidence of Islam to people so that the truth can be differentiated from falsehood. Islam is clear in terms of its Message and Mission, which no one is compelled to accept. Those not stubborn or arrogant will believe and accept Islam, and whoever rejects the truth may do so of their own free will. No one can threaten or harm anyone because they choose not to accept Islam. If one is compelled to take this faith, they are not truly Muslim. A Muslim must submit *voluntarily* to God.

Islam does not allow the fighting of non-combatants. Military conflicts should be lodged against only fighting soldiers, not against innocent civilians. For example, acts such as those committed on that dreaded day of 9/11 in the United States are classified as major sins in Islam and carry the death penalty.

"…Whoever kills a soul unless for a soul or corruption done in the land —it is as if he had slain mankind entirely. And whoever saves one – it is as if he had saved mankind entirely…" (Quran 5:32)

It is also forbidden for one to harm or kill oneself by any means. Suicide is a severe sin in Islam, a state of disbelief and loss of faith the Holy Quran condemns.

"… do not throw yourselves with your own hands into destruction. And do good; indeed, Allah loves the doers of good" (Quran 2:195)

Unfortunately, as in the case with all other major religions, brainwashed Muslim youth are drafted into misguided terrorist groups, believing they will die as martyrs and go directly to Paradise through suicide bombings. Islam condemns suicide in any form. If attacked, one may fight back in self-defense. Muslims should be keen to defend themselves and preserve their own lives.

"Permission to fight has been given to those who are being fought because they were wronged. And indeed, Allah is competent to give them victory" (Quran 22:39)

If the opposing party refrains from aggression and offers peace, Muslims are expected to return their hand in a matching gesture of peace.

"And if they incline to peace, then incline to it also and rely upon Allah. Indeed, it is He who is the Hearing, the Knowing" (Quran 8:61)

The first battle fought by our Prophet PBUH and his followers, the Battle of Badr, was an act of defense against a group that plotted and waged war against them. When fighting in defense, the Holy Quran warns Muslims not to exceed their military actions beyond the proper limits.

"Fight in the way of Allah those who fight you but do not transgress. Indeed. Allah does not like transgressors" (Quran 2:190)

This type of fighting is permitted, as it is a lesser evil designed to rid the world of a bigger evil. It is committed to enjoin the right and forbid the wrong. It constitutes the act of fighting to defend Islam rather than spreading it. Islam has provided specific guidelines for fighting against the enemy in self-defense and allows only fighting with minimum necessary force. It prohibits killing children, women, the elderly, the sick, monks in monasteries, rabbis, those sitting in places of worship, and the murder of any other non-combatant, even in a state of war.

Islam does not allow the torture of prisoners of war, mutilation, treason, rape, cutting down of fruitful trees, destroying cultivated fields or gardens, or destroying property. Islam also does not allow the slaughter of cows, sheep, and camels, except for food. Muslims are also forbidden from attacking wounded soldiers unless the wounded soldier acts violence against them.

Some enemies of Islam take the text of the Holy Quran and Hadith out of context, claiming that Islam promotes violence and terrorism. However, true Jihad has nothing to do with harming oneself or society. Jihad remains a noble matter and—when enacted--represents a noble strike for the sake of and in the name of God.

Understanding Jizya, and is it a Non-Muslim Tax?

"Fight those who do not believe in Allah and the Last Day, nor comply with what Allah and His Messenger have forbidden, nor embrace the religion of truth from among those who were given the Scripture, until they pay the tax, willingly submitting, fully humbled" (Quran 9:29)

There is wisdom and logic behind the concept of Jizya. The word *Jizya* is derived from the word *Jaza*, which translates to mean compensation. Jizya was a form of compensation or payment to the Islamic State for its public services rendered to non-Muslims living under Islamic rule. All states need funding to run their organized government, which is why all nations today level taxes against their citizens. Funding goes to support public services like police, military protection, welfare services, and more to help protect citizens' lives, families, property, and wealth.

In an Islamic state, Muslim citizens pay Zakat as their tax. Zakat stands as one of the five pillars of Islam, one that goes to help less fortunate citizens and supports the welfare system. Zakah is obligatory for Muslims so that a certain amount of their wealth will be contributed to the welfare of the poor. Zakah is a form of worship. Non-Muslims, on the other hand, cannot be forced to engage in religious obligations such as paying this Zakat—as it is a form of worship, and compulsory payment would infringe on non-muslims' religious rights.

Non-Muslims living under Muslim rule are free to practice their own religion in any Muslim land without being forced into any form of Islamic practice. But since non-Muslims also reap the social benefits of services provided by their Islamic host state, it is only fair that they pay a tax similar to that paid by their Muslim neighbors—identical to those taxes paid in all countries today. It would be an act of injustice towards Muslims to require them to pay a tax and not to require non-Muslims living in the same land to pay a share too.

Honoring and upholding treaties with non-Muslims is a solemn obligation for the Muslim community. The payment of Jizya ensures that the Islamic State protects and guards non-Muslim citizens against harassment from external enemies and funds any ransom imposed on their behalf if they are taken as captives by an external enemy.

Suppose that the Islamic State fails to protect or fears they cannot guarantee security for the non-Muslims living in their land as imposed by an external enemy. In that case, they will return the Jizya paid by the non-Muslims. This happened when Umar the Second Caliph ordered the treasury officer to refund Jizya collected from Syrian Christians because he feared he could not protect them from a military attack by the Byzantines.

Unlike countries today that charge taxes to all citizens, Jizya is not paid by all non-Muslim citizens but only by men of sound mind and of military age who are healthy and capable of earning a living. Women, children, the poor, students, the blind, the disabled, enslaved people, monks, the elderly, and those who chose to fight in the military were exempt from paying this tax. On the other hand, Zakat is paid for by Muslim men and women, but Muslim men cannot be exempt from being drafted into the military. Still, the Jizya payment exempts non-Muslims from joining the military even though the state's military benefits Muslims and non-Muslims alike. The Jizya paid by non-Muslims is generally less than what Muslims pay for Zakat.

The Islamic State is required to provide social security services to non-Muslims with disabilities who cannot work. There have been many instances where Muslims provided social security services to non-Muslim citizens living in their land.

It's important to mention that in an Islamic state, non-Muslims can observe the civil law prescribed by their own religious scriptures in matters such as marriage and divorce and others, and they are allowed to practice those acts and rituals that they consider permissible, such as eating pork and drinking wine. Furthermore, non-Muslims living under Muslim rule have the right to work, housing, education, transportation, religious centers, etc., just like Muslims.

If a non-Muslim resident refuses to pay the Jizya, consequences would be imposed on them, similar to the consequences faced by citizens who don't pay taxes to their government today—they often face criminal penalties. Jizya is not collected in modern Muslim nation-states and hasn't been accrued since the 19th century.

Is the Punishment for Apostasy Death in Islam?

A common misconception regarding Islam is that if someone leaves the religion of Islam, an Islamic State will punish them with death. This is simply not true. People always have the option to cease believing in and worshipping Allah in a Muslim land without being punished. Many people who left the religion of Islam in Muslim-dominated countries did so without being harmed. And many places of worship of other faiths can be found in Islamic countries today and in the past.

"And say, O Prophet, 'This is the truth from your Lord. Whoever wills let them believe, and whoever wills let them disbelieve..."
(Quran 18:29)

Islam clearly states that there is no compulsion regarding religion; therefore, an Islamic State cannot force anyone to convert to the Islamic faith or remain Muslim. The Holy Quran states:

"Let there be no compulsion in religion, for the truth stands out clearly from falsehood. So whoever renounces false gods and believes in Allah has certainly grasped the firmest, unfailing hand-hold. And Allah is All-Hearing, All-Knowing" (Quran 2:256)

It's essential to stress that the act of leaving the Islamic faith is not the same as committing the act of apostasy in Islam. Whereas Islam does state that the punishment for apostasy is death, this penalty is assigned only to a particular type of apostasy: and one does not suffer this penalty simply because they left the fold of Islam. The act of apostasy, the commission of which can sentence an apostate to death, is given to those living in an Islamic land that publicly announces their apostasy, convincing others to leave Islam, the religion of God. It's for those who call others to a new faith, misguiding people and leading them to hellfire, thus also leading to a great fitnah, trial, and tribulation for others.

The rights of an individual do not trump the rights of society. Islam does not tolerate the commission of any corruption in its society and has rules to protect the community from harm and disunity--and from those that cause doubt and uncertainty in the hearts of believers. Calling people to leave Islam can cause people to commit crimes prohibited in Islam, such as drinking alcohol, drugs, fornication, and other harmful acts to individuals and society. Apostacy, in short, is seen as a form of treason against the state.

The Islamic penal system aims to preserve five essential elements: life, intellect, family, property, and religion. To this end, Islam has implemented strict rules to live by through its religion and the prescription of the punishment for apostasy for the safety of society. Only an Islamic state can implement the punishment of apostasy; citizens cannot be vigilantes and take the law into their own hands. The crime must be done intentionally and implicitly, and not ambiguously.

At the time of Prophet Muhammad PBUH, apostates did exist, but Prophet Muhammad PBUH and the Muslims never executed any of them. Rarely have apostasy laws ever been implemented at all throughout history. The apostasy law is not unique to Islam; it also exists in Christianity and Judaism. A ruler in an Islamic State can elect to give the apostate a different sentence, such as a prison sentence. The apostate has the right to a court hearing and gets a three-day waiting period. He is allowed time to reflect on the situation, clear misconceptions, and repent. Those who assist the enemy of an Islamic State in battle are likewise subject to the death penalty. This is known as treason, and many nations today punish spies and anyone who plots to harm their own nation by way of their treason laws.

Does Islam Allow Slavery?

The Treatment of Female Prisoners of War

When speaking about slavery, we must define the term to ensure clarity and understanding. This is important because the Islamic term "slavery" differs from the Western definition of the word, as it holds a different connotation in the English language than in Islam. The term slavery in the West is more closely associated with brutal depictions seen in Hollywood movies and disturbing accounts found in the annals of American history.

When European settlers first arrived in America at the beginning of the 16th century, they abducted and enslaved approximately 11 million Africans for 300 years to work under abhorrent, inhumane conditions, generating wealth and opportunity for the American people. At the same time, two million enslaved people died at sea on their way to America. The Islamic term slavery does not reference such abhorrent conditions. Never would Islam allow such horrific treatment of human beings.

This brings us to the Islamic understanding of slavery. There was a time in history when slavery was not considered immoral, and almost every middle-class family owned a slave. They would kidnap free people from other lands and sell them into slavery. The act of enslaving people was a common practice in many areas. At a time when the inability to pay off one's debt could result in the enslavement of the debtor, Islam was the only religion to prohibit this form of practice and initiate laws about slavery.

Islam states that all human beings are free and that no human has the right to withhold freedom from anyone unlawfully. Therefore, Islam did not allow free people to be taken, sold, or turned into enslaved people. It prohibited all forms of slavery except for instances in which captives of war were claimed, an act having nothing to do with race or skin color.

To reaffirm, the only type of slavery Islam allowed was the taking of prisoners of war during the fighting of a battle. If two tribes were at battle and one side reigned victorious, taking enemy soldiers and citizens as captives of war, they could keep them. In modern times, soldiers of the opposite side can be imprisoned if captured because we now have prison institutions to house thousands of prisoners of war when needed.

However, back in the Prophet Muhammad PBUH's time, such institutions did not exist. At that time, prisoners of war would be killed, ransomed, or taken into homes as enslaved people. Instead of killing them, Islam allowed them to live humanely in the homes of Muslims without any form of abuse. The faith initiated laws dealing with prisoners of war that were not ransomed.

For those offended by the concept of wartime imprisonment: What else would Muslims have done with the prisoners they captured, enemies who had tried to fight and kill them? If they released them, those people could make another attempt on their lives. They didn't have prisons then, and even if they had housed captives of war, the prisoners would have lived in a harsher environment, especially when kept in the desert. Islamic scholars state that the law regarding treating war captives no longer applies today.

Whereas Islam allowed only the taking of prisoners of war, the faith did not abruptly abolish slavery altogether, commanding everyone who had slaves to release them. Islam decreased the practice of slavery by degrees to maintain social and economic stability. If everyone freed their slaves simultaneously, the act would have negatively affected their economy and society, putting thousands of people out of work without shelter. Islam encouraged and offered many avenues for people to release their slaves. Islam mandated freeing enslaved people as a requirement for forgiveness for specific sins. The Holy Quran referenced the freeing of an enslaved person as a sign of piety.

Numerous Ahadeeth (sayings of Prophet Muhammad PBUH) taught the humane way of treating enslaved people. This was unheard of at a time when other cultures did not have laws regulating the treatment of war captives and slaves, and they even would lend their female slaves to others for a night in exchange for a profit.

Islam allowed military commanders to exchange their captives for the other tribe's captives that were in battle with them or ransom them. Islamic law states that one cannot physically or sexually abuse a slave. If one harms or slanders a slave, he must set them free. One cannot force a slave to perform tasks that they cannot bear or that are too difficult for them. Islamic law required the master to clothe, feed, and house them as they would their families and to treat the slaves humanely as if they were their brothers and sisters.

Prophet Muhammad PBUH stated: *Your slaves are brothers of yours. Allah has placed them in your hand, and he who has his brother under him, he should feed him with what he eats, and dress him with what he dresses himself, and do not burden them beyond their capacities, and if you burden them, (beyond their capacities), then help them (Sahih Muslim 1661).*

This brings us to the matter of the treatment of female prisoners of war and the permissibility of marrying them. Islam prohibited killing female captives of war, substituting the slaying with enslavement, and even allowed the master to marry female prisoners of war. Although this mandate is no longer practiced today, Islam allowed the practice in the past for a necessary reason.

To fully understand this concept, put yourself in the shoes of people who lived more than 1400 years ago. This was at a time when women dressed in their best finery to go to the battlefield with their families, just in case their men lost, and they needed to go to the winning side. This warped tradition might sound harsh, but this was the reality for women of this time.

If women and children remained on the battlefield after the defeat of their people, when their husbands had been killed or escaped battle, the victors would come and claim them. Islam allowed this because if the Muslims did not take them, another tribe would come by and take the wives and kids and likely mistreat them. Islam allowed marriage and intercourse with female captives because the prohibition of these acts would deny these female captives their conjugal rights. Women, like men, have needs; the human desire for sexual fulfillment must be met, or the impact on the female body could be problematic.

Islam does not allow a master to abuse or rape women, and the Holy Quran prohibits masters from prostituting slaves. If the female captive of war is captured with her husband, she may not be taken as a concubine of her captor. If a child is born from a female prisoner, they are treated like a child born from a traditional marriage and cannot be born into slavery, as was done in Arabia before Islam. The slave mother's status also would be upgraded in that the master would not be able to sell her to anyone, and she would be freed if the baby's father died.

Those offended by the concept of enslaving female captives of war need to ask themselves where else people would have placed their female prisoners of war at that time. As stated, they didn't have prisons then. Islamic law mandates that if a slave requests a contract to repurchase themselves by working for a particular period or paying the master a specified monetary price to be freed, the master must honor it. This means the master would have to allow the slave to work and earn money. If a slave wants to marry another slave, the master must facilitate the marriage.

It's important to realize that, before modern times, no one criticized Islam regarding the treatment of captives of war because this treatment is not unjust. Enslaving an enemy that tried to kill you in battle is the lesser evil when compared to taking his life. Christians and Jews also had no issue with these laws regarding prisoners of war because they held similar laws for war captives during battle.

The Biblical narrative states that Prophet Abraham PBUH took Hagar as his concubine because his wife was barren. Some Christian scholars believe that he took her as a wife. The Old and New Testaments also don't prohibit or denounce slavery in general and sometimes go as far as to endorse it. According to the New Testament, Jesus Christ tells his people to fulfill the law until the Heavens and Earth meet their end. Islam, as stated, does not allow any act of slavery, except for the taking of prisoners of war, unlike Christianity and Judaism.

There are now people of a liberal belief system who think that taking captives of war throughout history was wrong, but they fail to consider the alternative. For example, would it have been logical to release those who tried to kill you and your family, allowing them an opportunity to strike again? Meanwhile, these liberals have no issues with what their government is doing today to attain political power, such as bombing other countries' innocent civilians and other horrid acts.

On the other hand, Islam does not allow the fighting of non-combatants. Islam does not allow the bombing of innocent civilians who are not soldiers fighting. Military conflicts should be directed against only fighting soldiers and not against innocent civilians. Islam does not allow the torture of prisoners of war, mutilation, treason, rape, cutting down of fruitful trees, destroying cultivated fields or gardens, or destroying property.

Islam also does not allow the slaughter of animals except for the cultivation of food. Muslims are also forbidden from attacking wounded soldiers unless the wounded soldier continues to fight them. Islam only mandates combat strategies with minimum necessary force, unlike what you see now in many countries. All Islamic laws are fair and ethical because they come directly from God--and God is All-Wise, All-Just.

The Verse of the Sword

"Kill Them Where You Find Them..." Verse

"So, when the sacred months expire, kill the polytheists wherever you find them, and catch them and besiege them and sit in ambush for them everywhere. Then, if they repent and establish Salāh and pay Zakāh, leave their way. Surely, Allah is most Forgiving, Very-Merciful" (Quran 9:5)

The Holy Quran was revealed to guide humanity through every aspect of life. It is an instructional manual that mandates just how one's life should be lived, with teachings for both individuals and all of society. The Holy Quran provides guidelines and instructions to govern proper human conduct, a fair economic system, ritual worship, ethics and moral behavior, business, government, and more. Among the many teachings include instruction on responding to hostile people during difficult times.

At age forty, Prophet Muhammad PBUH received his first Revelation from God in a cave via the Angel Gabriel. Although he was known in his community as "the truthful, the trustworthy," most people did not believe him or his Message. Even though Prophet Muhammad PBUH was spreading the Message of Islam to his people peacefully and did not force anyone to convert, a massive campaign was instigated by the idol worshippers of Mecca to persecute him and those who believed in the Message.

They harassed the Muslims, ridiculed and insulted them, socially boycotted and isolated them, threatened their lives, and even tortured certain believers to death. After thirteen years of preaching in Mecca while being persecuted, Prophet Muhamad PBUH and his followers secretly migrated to Medina, leaving family members, homes, and businesses behind.

In Medina, Prophet Muhammad PBUH gained new followers and became the city's leader. The idol worshippers of Mecca, who prosecuted Muslims in their homeland, plotted and attempted to reengage their attack. Thus the Muslims prepared for battle to defend themselves and their families from the oppressors that had expelled them from their homes in Mecca. A number of years and several battles later, Prophet Muhammad PBUH led an army of one hundred thousand people back to Mecca and conquered the land in a bloodless victory.

Prophet Muhammad PBUH gathered the chief enemies that had been battling him through the years and told them, *"I say to you what my brother Yusuf said to his unkind brothers. Have no fear this day! May Allah forgive you, and He is the Most Merciful."*

The Holy Quran was not revealed in a single setting; it was revealed to Prophet Muhammad PBUH passage by passage over 23 years. At this time, a Verse was revealed to Prophet Muhammad PBUH saying to give the criminal polytheists who broke their treaties with the Muslims, fighting them through the years despite signing peace treaties, a safe place where they could be unthreatened and not intimidated by the Muslims. God stated that they get four months to consider the religion of Islam.

"And if anyone from the polytheists asks for your protection (O Prophet), grant it to them so they may hear the Word of Allah, then escort them to a place of safety, for they are a people who have no knowledge" (Quran 9:6)

The desired outcome was for these criminals to become Muslims, but if they chose not to convert, they would be required to leave the area. Upon the completion of the four months, if they didn't depart, the command was to *"kill them where you find them."* The Muslims were instructed to drive out these criminal idol worshippers from the very land that had forced out the Muslims. This is the precise context of the Verse as delivered.

This Verse references a specific treaty given to the idol worshippers of Mecca from God. While the directive is intended to threaten the idol worshippers that expelled the Muslims from Mecca, not a single person died because of this Verse. At that time, public idol worship was no longer allowed in Arabia. As a result, paganism disappeared throughout the land of Arabia.

Another Verse states that if any polytheist should seek protection from the Muslims, they must grant them protection so they might hear Allah's Message. If the polytheist did not convert, the Muslims would escort them to the borders and release them. The Muslims were only permitted to kill those criminal polytheists who refused to leave the land-- the very land they initially forced out the Muslims.

It's imperative to emphasize that these Verses and commands are not instructions to govern the actions of Muslims today. Instead, these words take the form of Verses from God that address specific people at a particular time. They pertained explicitly to those idol worshippers that broke their treaties with Prophet Muhammad PBUH and the Muslims, who had been attacking them in violation of their signed peace treaty.

If Muslims were ordered to kill non-Muslims, you would not have found so many Christians and Jews living in an Islamic land throughout history. Muslims have always been directed to allow non-Muslims to live in peace, kindness, and mercy. This, in truth, is the Muslim way.

Why are There Two Sects of Muslim?

What is the Difference Between Sunni and Shia?

Two separate branches of Muslim predominate this faith. 90% of the Muslim world is Sunni, and 8% is Shia in faith. The followers of Shia are commonly found in Iran, Iraq, Lebanon, Bahrain, and a few other places. The difference between Sunni and Shia arose because of a political division at the time in history when Shia followers went their separate way. Yet, while the split started as a difference of opinion in politics, some significant theological differences emerged later, with Shia incorporating many unconventional, foreign concepts into their theology.

The Sunni and Shia split found its origin in a disagreement about the leadership of the Muslim community after the death of Prophet Muhammad PBUH. After his death, his companions were forced to choose the next leader, the ruler, and the successor of the Muslim community, commonly known as the Caliphate. Sunnis believed that Prophet Muhammad PBUH did not explicitly designate his replacement, and they needed to appoint this leader by mutual consultation. The Shia believed that the Prophet PBUH designated his cousin and son-in-law, Ali PBUH, to assume the role of Caliph.

Sunni Muslims deemed Abu Bakr R.A., the Prophet's closest companion, as the fittest to lead the Muslim community. Abu Bakr became the first Caliph, and Ali eventually became the fourth, serving in the wake of Abu Bakr, Umar, and Uthman, peace be upon them. Ali was well-satisfied with the decision to appoint Abu Bakr R.A. as the ruler, but others were less pleased.

The word *Sunni* comes from the term *Sunnah,* which refers to the teachings and practice of Prophet Muhammad PBUH, who in turn was taught by Angel Gabriel—who, for his part, learned the faith from God. Sunni Muslims consider themselves followers of Islam's orthodox tradition, adhering to the pure, uninfluenced faith taught by Prophet Muhammad PBUH. Shia linguistically means party, sect, supporters, or a group of similar-minded people. *Shia* is an abbreviation for *Shiatu Ali,* which signifies *a group or supporters of Ali.* Shia was a political faction that claimed the cousin and son-in-law of Prophet Muhammad, PBUH, should lead the Islamic community as the Caliphate in place of Abu Bakr R.A.

Initially, this group of Ali's supporters, known as Shia, stood against the Umayyads political party but remained purely Sunni in their theology and faith, unlike modern-day Shia. Yet, with passing years, significant doctrine/theological differences arose. The famous 12 Imams that certain Shia holds in the highest regard were Sunni in Creed, not Shia.

If Prophet Muhammad PBUH explicitly appointed Ali PBUH, as the Shia claim, that would mean Abu Bakr was appointed unjustly in the role of a caliph. It means he disobeyed and went against the wishes of the Prophet, PBUH, despite his role as his closest associate and dearest friend. Additionally, this move implied that the companions who accepted Abu Bakr R.A. as the Caliphate went against the Prophet PBUH despite earning a high rank and God's praise in the Holy Quran.

Many beliefs of Shiism claim no basis in the religion of Islam. Shiism evolved from its role as a political sect supporting and favoring the leadership of Ali and his descendants, who they label as Imams, over more qualified companions, to a holder and conveyor of strange ideas foreign to Islam.

Among the most significant differences between Sunni and Shia is that the mainstream Shia upholds the divinity of 12 imams to which they ascribe powers, privileges, and attributes that belong only to Allah, the Glorious. Some Shia believes these 12 Imams to be infallible and incapable of committing an error. It is believed that they are all-knowledgeable, all-powerful, perfect, possessing supernatural powers, and stand in control of the Universe and all of creation. They believe these 12 Imams are superior to and hold a higher rank than Prophets. Sunnis, of course, don't believe any of this.

Shia also directs many acts of worship to these imams, ranging from supplications to sacrifices and seeking their aid. These acts contradict Islam's central teaching, which states that only Allah is worthy of worship and veneration. The act of ascribing partners to Allah is the biggest sin in Islam and the only sin God would not forgive if one died in that state without repenting.

"...Indeed, he who associates others with Allah - Allah has forbidden him Paradise, and his refuge is the Fire. And there are not for the wrongdoers any helpers" (Quran 5:72)

While Shia considers Ahlul Bayt (the family of Prophet Muhammad PBUH) above and beyond everyone else in a supernatural, divine way, Sunnis only highly respect the Muslims of them-- considering them righteous but ascribing no divine powers to them--as they were only humans and thus unworthy of the worship and veneration owed to Allah alone.

Another bizarre belief of some Shia is that they do not deem many of the Sahabah (the companions of Prophet Muhammad PBUH) true Muslims, including the famous Sahabah. They consider them to be defectors from the folds of Islam. Shia bears hate and animosity toward the Sahabah and even slander them. They claim that only seven of these companions stayed within the folds of Islam, with the rest qualifying as disbelievers or hypocrites.

The Holy Quran affirms the virtue and status of the companions of the Prophet, declaring Allah the Glorious was pleased with them. Shiites reject the Sunnah (the tradition, teachings, and practice of the Prophet PBUH) because the Prophet's companions passed down these teachings to the next generations. Sunnis respect and love all of the Prophet's companions, including Ali and his two sons, Hassan and Hussein, peace be upon them.

Another significant difference between Sunni and Shia beliefs lies in the Shiite's claim that the Holy Quran of our time is deficient and has not been preserved properly. The Shia believe in a book called the "Tablet of Fatimah," which is supposedly three times longer than the Holy Quran. They claim that this book was revealed to Fatimah, the daughter of the Prophet, after his death and referenced the upcoming Imams. The Shia believe this Book is held by the Mahdi, who has been in hiding for the past 900 years and will come forth to present its text at the end of times. They believe the Mahdi is Ali.

Sunnis believe in the One and Only Holy Quran, revealed to Prophet Muhammad PBUH as the last and final Scripture to humanity, the same One read by hundreds of millions of Muslims around the globe, that contains the verbatim word of God and will never change. The Holy Quran states that God took it upon Himself to preserve and safeguard His Final Book from any man-made modifications, such as those made to the previous Books, the Gospel, and the Torah.

"Indeed, it is We who sent down the Qur'an and indeed, We will be its guardian" (Quran 15:9)

When Ali became the 4th Caliph, his sons, Hassan and Hussain, were in attendance to learn from and assist their father, having stood beside him in three battles. Ali R.A. was ultimately assassinated by a group of misguided people known as the Khawarij. After his death, Hassan, Ali's older son and the Prophet's older grandson was given the oath of allegiance by the people of Kufa in Iraq. Simultaneously, the people of Syria gave Mu'awiyah the oath of allegiance. For the first time in Islamic history, two Caliphates presided at once.

When Hassan and Mu'awiyah were poised to return to battle, Hassan resigned after six months and moved to Madinah, as he disliked fighting and bloodshed. He resigned for the sake of unity, although he stood as the more righteous and qualified Caliphate candidate. Hassan swore allegiance to Mu'awiyah, pledging to listen to and obey him, providing that he ruled according to the Book of Allah and the teachings of Prophet Muhammad PBUH. There followed in the wake of this allegiance 20 years of peace. Hassan fulfilled the prophecy of Prophet Muhammad PBUH when he stated, *Indeed, this son of mine is a chief; Allah shall bring peace between two Muslim parties through his hands.* Note: Our Prophet PBUH referred to both armies as Muslim in faith.

Hassan later passed away. Then, as the death of the Caliph Mu'awiyah loomed imminently, he appointed his son, Yazid, to succeed him, even though Hussein, the Prophet's younger grandson, was more righteous and overall more qualified to become the Caliphate. The governor of Medina called Hussein to his house and insisted that he give the Oath of Allegiance in public. Hussein repeatedly refused. The people of Kufa barraged Hussein with letters, asking him to appear before them to accept their vow of allegiance, acknowledging him instead as their ruler and the next Caliph.

They promised to support him. In response, Hussein sent his cousin out among the people on a scouting mission, curious to see if the people of Kufa were serious in their intent. Later, his cousin wrote a letter to Hussein, summoning him to come immediately as the tribes of Kufa sent 12,000 members, each representing a tribe, to offer their oath of allegiance.

Wise men who loved Hussein begged him not to go, but Hussein insisted. When he arrived at Karbala, his followers abandoned him. Only about 4,000 of the promised 12,000 representatives came to offer their oath. His scouting cousin was murdered. And ultimately, Hussein was killed wrongfully and died as a martyr. Once Yazid heard the news of Hussein's death, he protested that his command to his minions had been a request to stop Hussein, not to kill him.

Islam and the Holy Quran command no sects nor divisions among Muslims. The Holy Quran states:

"And hold firmly to the rope of Allah all together and do not become divided..." (Quran 3:103)

The word "rope" here refers to the Holy Quran. Muslims are avowed to unite as one under the Message of the Holy Quran and the Sunnah.

"Verily, those who divide their religion and break up into sects, you have no concern in them in the least. Their affair is only with Allah, who then will tell them what they used to do"
(Quran 6:159)

Followers of the Sunni ideology use the word Sunni not to divide the ummah (Islamic community) but to differentiate themselves from certain sects that have emerged and developed independently, finding no basis in our religion. After the death of Prophet Muhammad PBUH, at the time of the Sahabah (companions of the Prophet), conflicts arose between Muslims. Certain small groups broke away and gained a different understanding of Islam. Some of these small new groups did not accept the Sunnah and Hadith, and some did not believe in predestination - all vital parts of Islam.

Sunnis practice Orthodox Islam, the way taught by our Prophet PBUH, and believe in the Holy Quran, Hadith, and predestination. Due to these new groups that are different in belief, Sunnis characterize and differentiate themselves so people will not misinterpret their mission and beliefs. Unfortunately, people with evil intentions misuse this term to divide Muslims and spread hate.

The most common form of Shiism today is Twelver Shiism, which beliefs in the twelve divine Imams. Another form of Shia is known as the Zaidis, who reject the concept of the Divine Imams and represent a minority sect of Shiites mainly found in Yemen. Many modern believers of Shia today are ignorant, blind followers of false faith. Instead of expressing hatred towards them, we should pray to God and ask Him to guide them on His pure, righteous path.

What is the Concept of Atonement in Islam? Is it Similar to That of Christianity? How Does One Seek Salvation from Hellfire & Enter Paradise?

Before we discuss the concept of atonement in Islam, it's essential to address Christianity's stance on how to seek salvation from hellfire and enter Paradise. Christians believe that every child is born with the taint of the original sin committed by our parents, Prophet Adam and Eve PBUT. The sin was committed when they disobeyed our Creator by eating from the forbidden tree. Christians believe that, since all men are born in a sinful state because of the actions of our distant ancestors, it is necessary to believe in atonement, the idea that Jesus Christ died for our sins. Christians believe that one can attain salvation, being saved from hellfire and entering Paradise, by simply accepting that Jesus Christ died for their sins, without the need for worshipping God, doing good deeds, or adhering to the Holy Law - because Jesus Christ fulfilled it for them.

To reiterate, Christians believe the commandments of God are worthless and need not be followed, as they can earn a free trip to Paradise by simply believing that Jesus Christ died for their sins. They believe one can live sinful without going to hell since Jesus Christ atoned for their sins. If all Christians need to do to reach Paradise is to believe that Jesus Christ died for their sins, then why do they bother learning the Bible or the teachings of Jesus Christ?

If Jesus Christ did die for our sins, he would have emphasized and taught this crucial detail. However, nowhere in the Bible did Jesus Christ explicitly stated that he would die to save humanity from sin. Christians say God sacrificed his only begotten son to save humanity, but if God owns the entire universe, why did God need to sacrifice Jesus? One sacrifices one thing for something else they could not obtain otherwise. But God is All-Mighty and can restore the life of Jesus Christ instantly, so by definition, that is not a sacrifice.

Not only is the concept of atonement not mentioned in the Bible nor taught by Jesus Christ, but Biblical verses contradict the concept of atonement and prove a fabrication. These verses state that no person is held responsible for another's sin, no parent is accountable for a sin committed by their child, and vice versa. That means we are not held accountable for the sins committed by our parents, Adam and Eve, PBUH.

"The fathers shall not be put to death for the children, neither shall the children be put to death for the fathers: every man shall be put to death for his own sin." (Deuteronomy 24:16). Take this passage: *"The child will not share the guilt of the parent, nor will the parent share the guilt of the child."* (Ezekiel 18:20) It is stated in the Bible that the child will not share the guilt of the parent for any particular sin, nor will the parent share the child's responsibility for a sin!

Paul initiated the concept of atonement. Paul proved himself an enemy of Jesus Christ throughout his ministry. He claimed that Jesus

Christ came to him in a dream, and only afterward did he become a believer. He then made radical changes to the religion that neither Jesus Christ nor the Bible describes or details! Why are Christians following the teaching of Paul and not Jesus Christ?

How did all of the previous, righteous Messengers and Prophets of God, such as Prophet Abraham, Moses, Noah, etc., go to Paradise if they did not accept Jesus Christ, one who did not die for their sins since he was not yet born, as their savior? Are these righteous Messengers and Prophets of God going to hell?! No, of course not! And why didn't these Messengers and Prophets of God know of or teach about the original sin and redemption? That's because these ideas were innovated by Paul and never taught by God, Jesus Christ, the Bible, or anyone.

When someone approached Jesus Christ and asked him what he must do to obtain eternal life, he mentioned nothing about atonement, nor did he state that the person must believe that Christ died for our sins. Instead, Jesus told him he must keep the commandments.

Let us review the conversation that took place between them: *"Just then a man came up to Jesus and asked, 'Teacher, what good thing must I do to get eternal life? Why do you ask me about what is good?' Jesus replied. 'There is only One who is good. If you want to enter life, keep the commandments." Which ones?' he inquired. Jesus replied, 'You shall not murder, you shall not commit adultery, you shall not steal, you shall not give false testimony, honor your father and mother and love your neighbor as yourself.' 'All these I have kept,' the young man said. 'What do I still lack?' Jesus answered, 'If you want to be perfect, go, sell your possessions and give to the poor, and you will have treasure in heaven. Then come, follow me.'"* (Matthew 19:16-21)

The Bible states that God's commandments are required for good living and must be followed; if anyone says otherwise, they will be called the least in the Kingdom of Heaven. *"For truly I tell you until heaven and earth disappear, not the smallest letter, not the least stroke of a pen, will by any means disappear from the Law until everything is accomplished. Therefore, anyone who sets aside one of the least of these commands and teaches others accordingly will be called least in the kingdom of heaven, but whoever practices and teaches these commands will be called great in the kingdom of heaven."* (Matthew 5:18-19)

What value is faith if you don't reinforce it with good deeds? asks the Bible, which contradicts what Christians believe today as they follow the teachings of Paul and not Jesus Christ. *"What good is it, my brothers and sisters, if someone claims to have faith but has no deeds? Can such faith save them?"* (James 2:14)

Some Christians believe that even infants will go to hell if they die without being baptized, as they were born with inherited sin and never accepted Jesus Christ as their savior. The Bible contradicts this, proving that children are not born in a sinful state and, therefore, can go to Paradise upon death. Jesus said, *"Let the little children come to me, and do not hinder them, for the kingdom of heaven belongs to such as these."* (Matthew 19:14). The idea that people are born sinful because of an act they did not commit is illogical; it is not like our All-Wise, Most-Merciful, Just God to enforce such a concept! Imagine a baby born in innocence, then dying a year later and going to hell. Where is the justice? It is not the duty of one soul to carry the burden of another, and no justice is to be found in the punishment of one person for saving another when they never sinned.

Now let's transition to Islam, which holds a true, logical, and simple concept of salvation. Islam teaches that everyone is responsible and will be held accountable for their own actions. Thus, everyone is responsible for their own salvation. The exempt are those who have not reached puberty and those not of sound mind. Unlike the teaching of Christianity, Islam does not indicate the presence of intermediaries between man and God, nor that sin is inherited or passed on to another. As no one will carry or atone for your sins for you, this means that you must strive to better yourself, build your connection with God and His Book, and follow His Commandments. Unlike Christian teaching, Islam teaches that attaining Paradise requires belief and work—not simply faith. The act of merely believing is not enough.

"Whoever chooses to be guided, it is only for their own good. And whoever chooses to stray, it is only to their own loss. No soul burdened with sin will bear the burden of another. And We would never punish a people until We have sent a messenger to warn them" (Quran 17:15)

Salvation comes only from believing in One God and following His commandments. One needs to believe in what God and His Messenger have taught us, which includes the Six Pillars of faith in Islam; the Belief in the Oneness of Allah, His Angels, His Prophets and Messengers, His Books, the Last Day/Judgement Day; and the Belief in Divine Predestination. One needs to follow the commandment of Allah, which includes the Five Pillars of Islam and Sharia (Islamic Law). One can gain Allah's Mercy by holding and following these beliefs to enter Paradise.

It's imperative to note that since God created human beings with free will and made them fallible and prone to mistakes, humans will slip up from time to time. The Holy Quran states that Allah taught Prophet Adam, PBUH, how to ask for forgiveness. When Prophet Adam, PBUH, ate from the forbidden tree, Adam, PBUH, acknowledged his mistake, experienced guilt, and asked for forgiveness. God, the Almighty, accepted his repentance without sacrificing the life of an innocent person. God is teaching Prophet Adam, PBUH, and us, by extension, what actions to take when we make a mistake. We can receive forgiveness for sins solely through sincere repentance, with this forgiveness sought directly from God.

"Then Adam received some words from his Lord, and He accepted his repentance. Indeed, it is He who is the Accepting of Repentance, the Merciful." (Quran 2:37)

God does not expect us to live without sinning. He created the Angels, who follow all of God's commandments and never disobey Him. But God also wanted to create humans who would submit to God by choice. Prophet Muhammad, PBUH, stated: *"Every son of Adam commits sin, and the best of those who sin are those who repent"* (Sunan Ibn Majah 4251). Humans have to struggle with their whims and desires, and they must also struggle with the intrusive whispers of Satan, who constantly tries to tempt them to sin, glamorizes sinful behavior, and deceives humanity to take them astray from the remembrance and obedience of God.

God promises to forgive all sins, no matter the size and number— even if the sin reaches the Heavens. His gate of repentance is always open to anyone until the sun rises from the west or until the person reaches death. So, when you sin, repent to your Lord! Allah loves those who repent and purify themselves. For your sin to be forgiven, you must regret your sinful actions, cease that sinful behavior, and commit from repeating it.

"But whoever repents after their wrongdoing and mends their ways, Allah will surely turn to them in forgiveness. Indeed, Allah is All-Forgiving, Most Merciful" (Quran 5:39)

It's important to note that the commission of good deeds alone is not enough to gain admittance into Paradise--and that it is only with God's Mercy that one enters Paradise. With the belief in and following of the One God, Allah, one can gain His Mercy to enter Paradise.

"Say, "O My servants who have transgressed against themselves by sinning, do not despair of the mercy of Allah. Indeed, Allah forgives all sins. Indeed, it is He who is the Forgiving, the Merciful" (Quran 39:53)

The Sincere Seeker's Introductory book to Islam,

'*The Sacred Path to Islam,*' and other Islamic books for adults and children are available on The Sincere Seeker's Amazon page www.amazon.com/thesincereseeker.

You are encouraged to visit and subscribe to The Sincere Seeker's Blog at www.TheSincereSeeker.com

and The Sincere Seeker's YouTube Channel www.youtube.com/c/TheSincereSeeker

Convert to Islam and Become Muslim in a 5-minute Call. Schedule your call here: https://www.thesincereseeker.com/convert-to-islam-and-become-muslim/

For questions or comments, please contact me at hello@thesincereseeker.com

www.ingramcontent.com/pod-product-compliance
Lightning Source LLC
Chambersburg PA
CBHW071158120626
46546CB00006B/2318